Element

An aspect; an element of danger

Elemental

Fundamental; related to embodying the powers of nature

Element

Constituent basic part

Elementary

Relating to the most rudimentary aspects of a subject

When I finished my last book *informal* I went for walks in the country and visited some strange places (even my back garden!) as part of a recovery process, bits of it caught by my camera. I also sketched when I could, notions of deeper patterns in what I saw. The idea of overlap of sketch and abstract with the literal picture took hold. I began a log. The merest trace, even a repeat motif of a picture, gave life to the mind to pattern. I took note: if only one knew how to look, not just at the landscape and its detail but also into the mantras of geometry and numbers, which help structure and organise. *Element* embraces such a world, artificial and natural. Fact and fiction mix. Which is which is hard to say after a time but it is to do with Pattern, that links eye to mind. And the reader is invited to go deeper, making the observations and speculation that enriches the Element. The smallest dot and dash begins the journey...

The thing is, what do I look at? On the surface, colours and the shape that greet me; but if I keep staring another picture enters, blurred, losing detail. Only certain features remain which give character, like a certain cast to the face or gleam in the eye. If I look further the focus leads to more loss, as if the retinal image cannot hold. Surprisingly, other shapes emerge. An inner eye engages and the spirit behind the body takes over. The snapshot is the first gateway; then a sketch takes me through the second, intent on character. Beyond this the deeper feature is caught only in a diagram, more a concept of the thing than the actuality. But through this third gateway the mind's eye switches on – in abstract readings. Something else is resurrected, stirring up emotions and memories. When word and line cease, visceral feelings make the forms beyond the shapes, hallucinatory, and poetic.

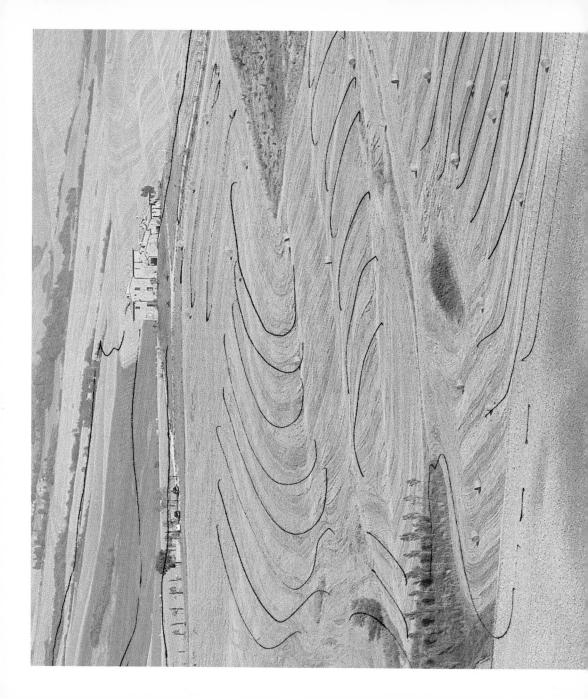

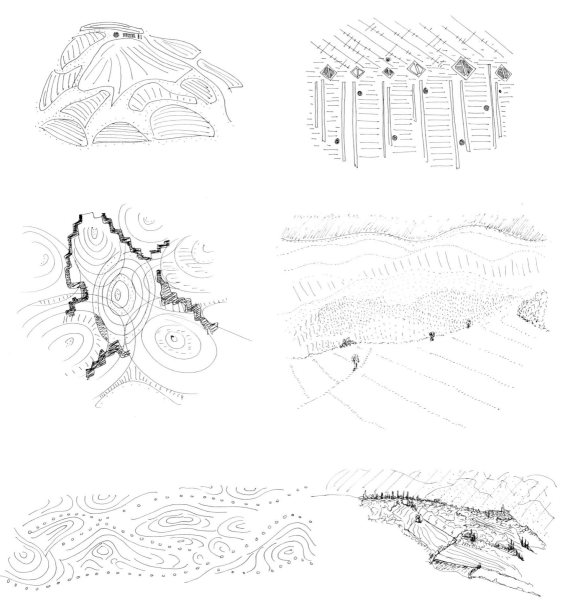

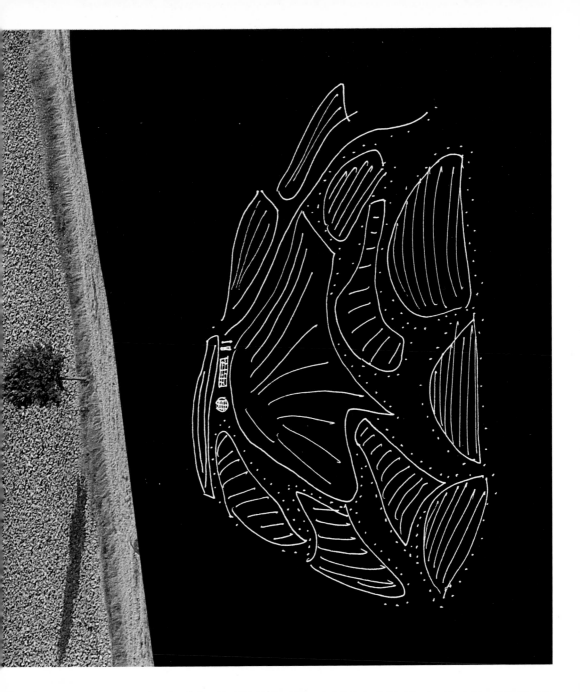

Tuscany
a scorched earth with bales and lines
– knots in wood and fine grain –
as drawn in timber.

10

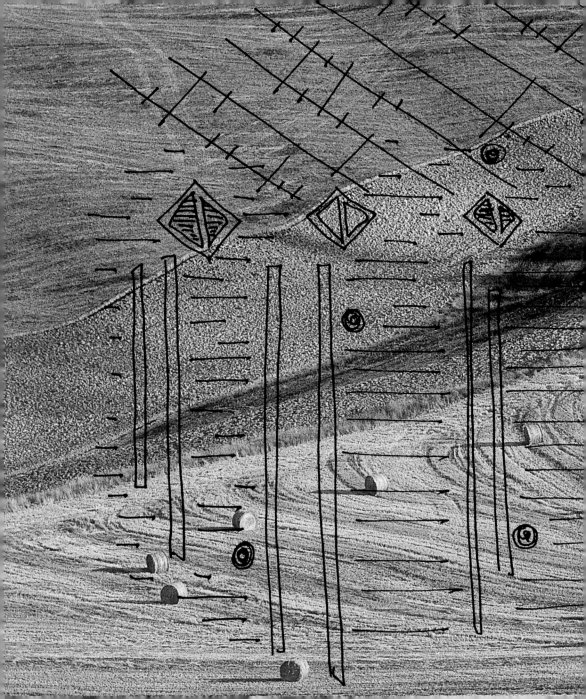

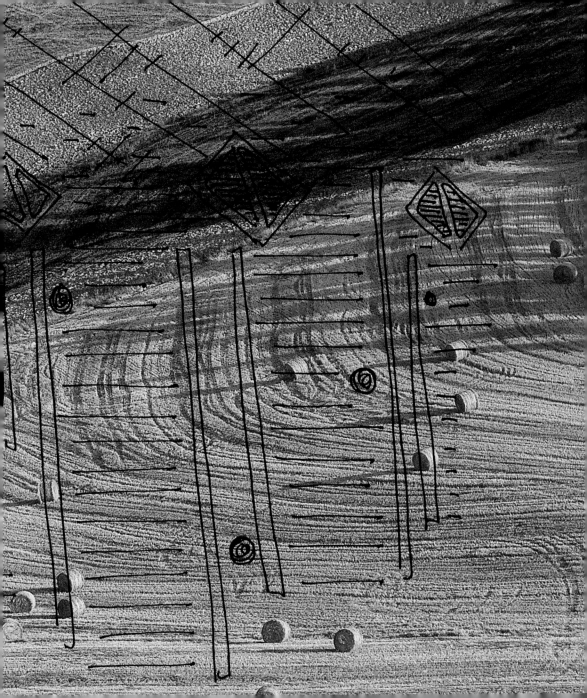

27

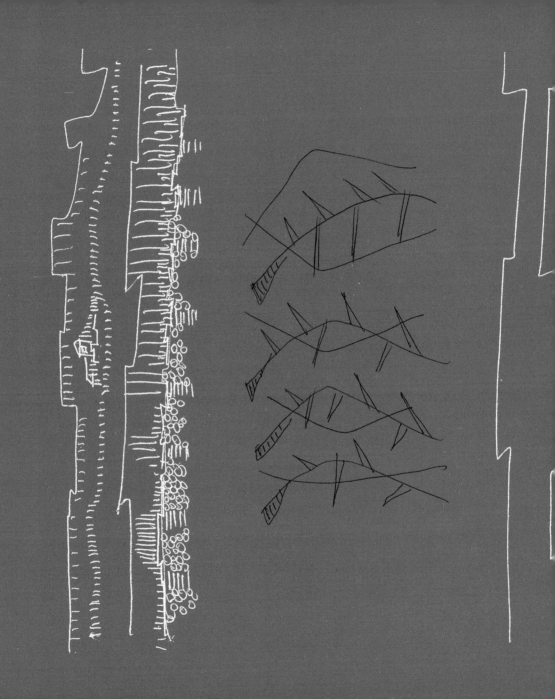

Sounds of breeze rustling
and blowing in the river
runs. At their edge an
underworld commences –
orange stems marking the
border. The reeds shoot up to
sieve the breeze and whistle
their heads of purple brown.
Above them long and low
the hedges stretch out the
middle distance; the fields
bank up to the horizon where
a bordering of trees holds
abrupt shadows. The motion
picks up, the wind's rush is
even faster, the mass hisses.

Nature could be an open book
on a day like this of almost
unbelievable innocence,
the stillness, the hedgerows
in lines, green fields, and a
sky with no clouds. But the
wind rises to say something
different. The reeds tremble,
day shifts. I look at the
lightness hurried away and a
disquiet sets in, a foreboding
that in the shadows belong
the unspeakable things.
Underneath the agitation,
within the grip of mud and
wet, there is a killing thread.

Nature comes upon us in many ways – beguiling, seductive, cruel. She cloaks herself in mists, soothing greens and sunsets of warm red welcome; she poses – we are taken in. A terrifying form then rips the heart out of the earth in jagged fractures, heaving the sea and wringing the sky to flood and destroy, attacking like a locust storm the thin foliage of our self-importance. Any thought of a benign presence is hard to hold on to. But just as we grid minds to believe again in our powers, we slip guard; and are overcome by the scent of flowers, the wind's rustle in the leaves, the taste of fruit, the soft touch of moss. Nature's sensuality invades effortlessly, impossible to stay outside. She embraces and smiles. We rush in. The earth blushes, the clouds dab powder onto stunning blue cheeks. Her garments of Winter/Summer/Autumn/Spring change colours – keep us guessing. We are the changelings in her spells, nurturing like incubi her moods and confessions. We are the nervous system of a great mystery.

molecule of light

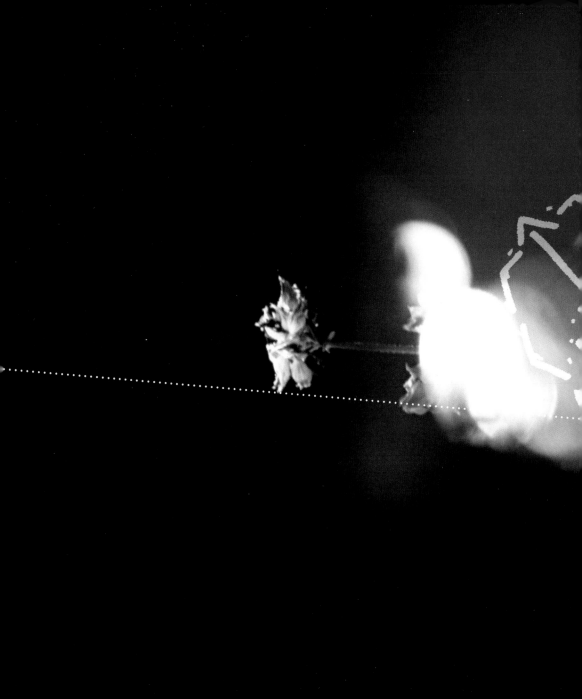

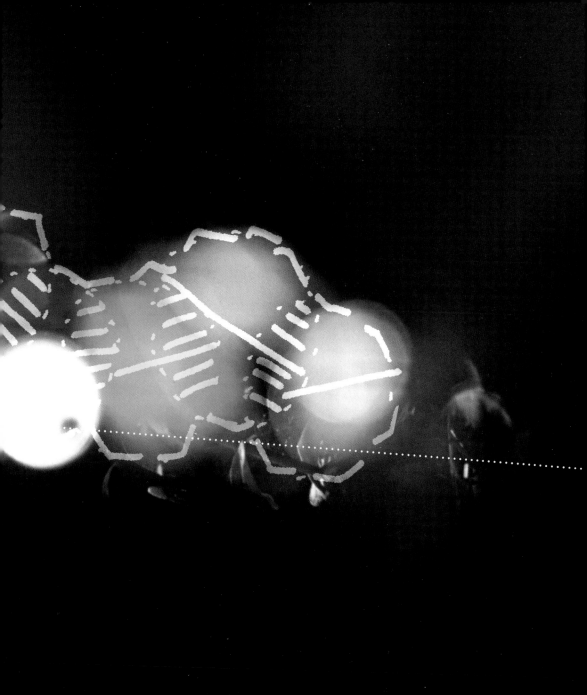

A molecule of light skips through – the fence stripes dark into
the earth. In between are gaps which catch slivers of plant in
long section: and fraction yellow flowers. Under a powerful lens,
a magnification of X20, the gaps turn into wide channels. Bits of
bud and petal swell with rapid circles, indistinct and overlapping.
They produce a daisy-chain of vibration. In calibration of air and
sunlight the colour molecule reveals its part-spectral structure
– white, green and yellow . . . .

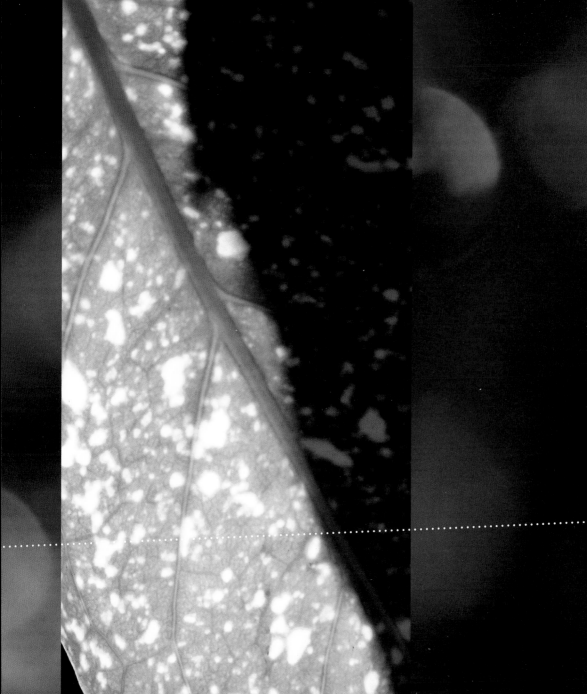

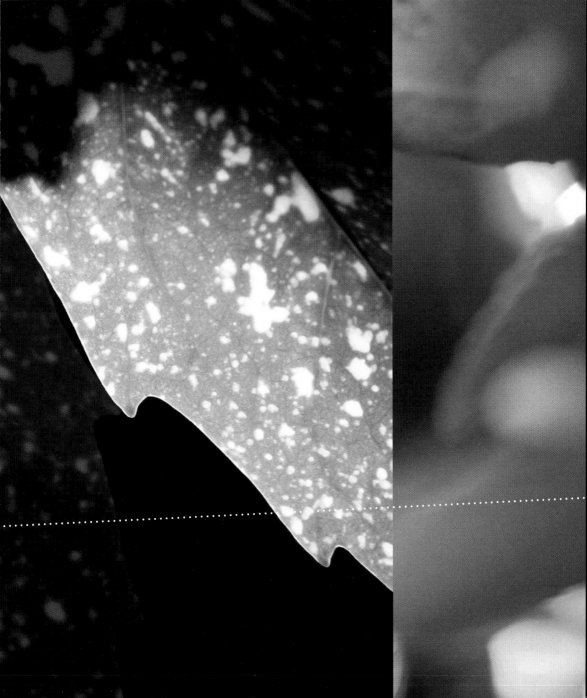

the branching turns in ever finer search, fractal like, to pattern a lung for air

Against the sun when a plant catches fire tiny veins etch and emboss
onto the leaf. What is coarse, the pulp of chlorophyll to the touch,
is shot through by rays – sun discs, scorched coals, cut diamonds
transform the tracery. The leaves flame with spirits. Sky searchlights
change descriptions and to transfigure becomes the rule of light.
Photons create stem and branch hallucinations . . . .

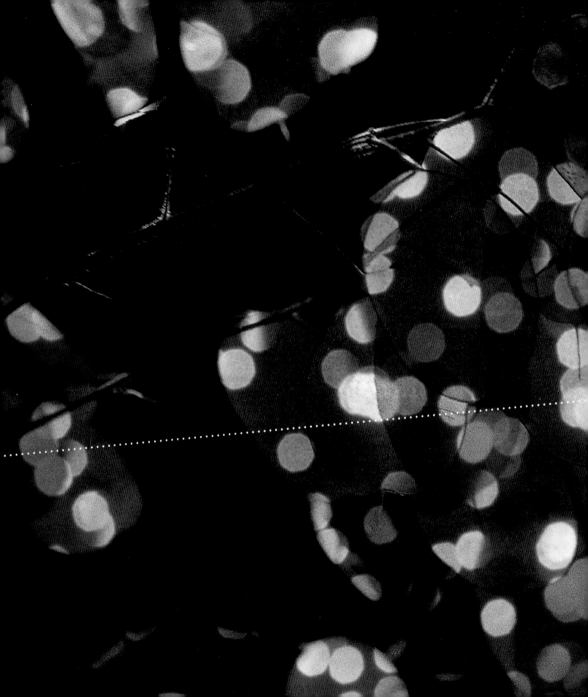

protoplasm chlorophyll

Tongues of fire have a special valency as they branch and lick at the air hungry for locations of oxygen; the surround is nothing but a generous offering that rushes in to fill the suction. The bonds that shape each tongue are the limits of combustion within the particular fields of carbon and nitrogen. To eat up the air is to branch out for breath. Phosphor on timber, the ignition sparks inert material to violence. Reds and yellow braid layers from slow burning to raging hot

At the base, hovering over the incendiary origin, each flame hides a blue space, a cool zone. Here is the strange thing of the source, that the root of incandescence harbours the coldest tone but the highest heat. The showy and flamier tips fan out to lower temperatures. Three colours balance the flames, blue, red and yellow – the fire molecule

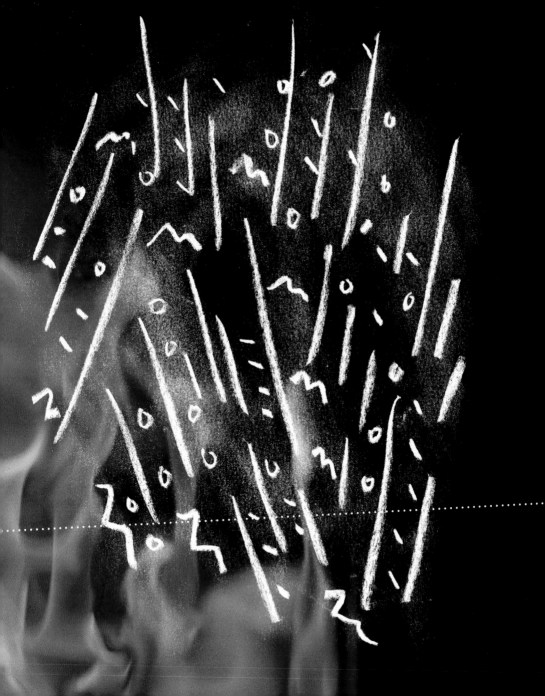

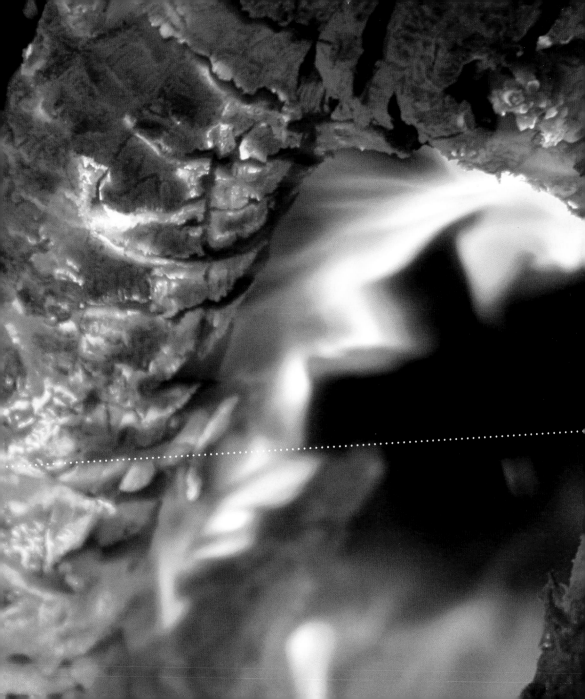

As the flame lives, so does the body that sustains it die, by degrees; a shadowy dance of embers that soon cremates the form. Only ash is left by the once-roaring tree. Combustion slow steps out to leave in the dark its sacrifice of rich carbon

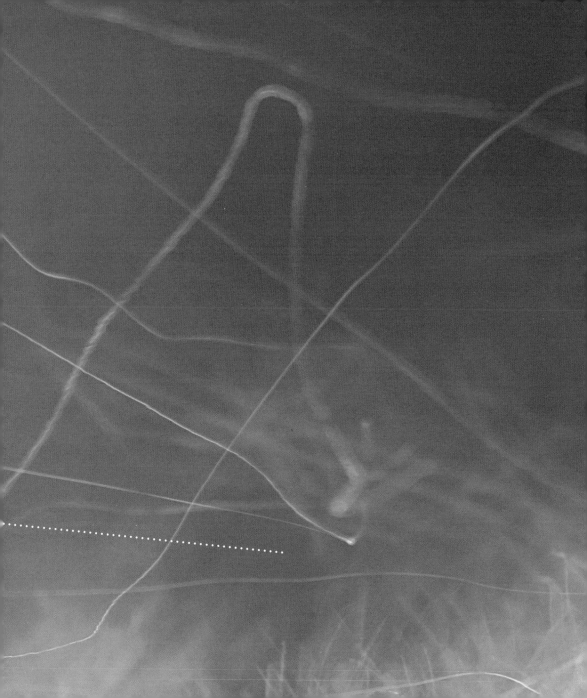

separate energies - crossing networks.

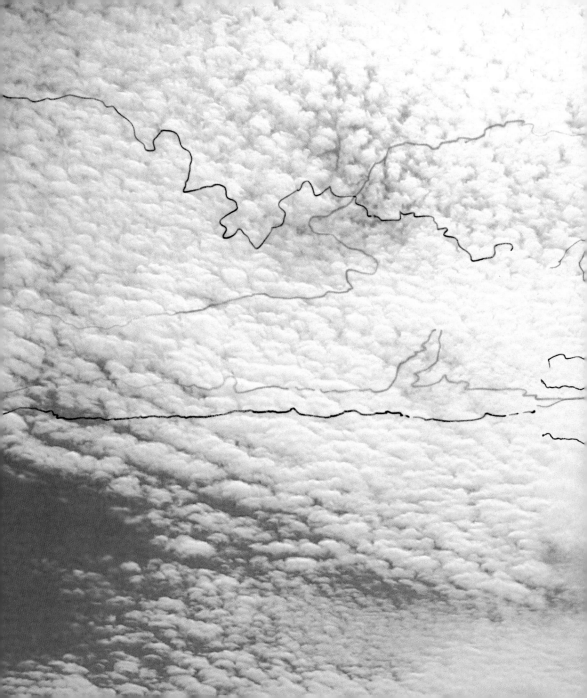

landscapes

coastlines

A journey that never ends, shape upon shape,
the frontiers a dashed line - moisture dots
pushed ahead by the wind. Slowed down by
friction the vapour takes body and packs
together in solid contour, mass and weight.
And the inertia moves across the sky in sheets,
puff balls or wispy filament. The constant act is
a forging of the heavens, making white with hope
or changing black to threaten and give fright.

In the depths of the mountainous mass there would be sheer drops into cataclysmic terror. The cliff faces, full of rain, are treacherous. Moisture crag and crevice bundle up one on the other, rising and towering to touch the source of lightning. From top to bottom a blanket weaves and tightens. As it gathers its heavy face the nature that cannot stay still will change. Rain will fall, from dark to light the features split. Fresh lips of sky beckon.

We take off from the ground into their element,
set our uncertain face to its whisper, and climb
farther into the fantastically wrought chambers.
Our hearts and minds go with these vessels,
reading their spells. Listen to the refraction of
the wind and the worship that never ends.

The sea along Big Sur is silver
threads and rolling green boulders.
In from a striking blue horizon that
sparkles the ocean colours green
entering the shallows, and the mass
turns from solid to shattering wave.
Rocks, blackened and eroded, stand
up to the onslaught and break the
flow. The agitation of channels
and circular motions start. White
braids stitch together; some spread
in shaky contour, others coalesce
making whirlpools and storms and
cataracts on the water.

The push of the sea stacks up in
cliffs, rising and cracking, loosening
boulders to stream down the water
face. Jagged crags form on the
sharp points. The sea is lifted solid
at this moment, a carving out of
ocean stone. Impossible to scale or
cling to, crushing if caught in the
mass of the downhill, water currents
spin in and out of avalanche.
Exhausted by the beach, foam
crackles and disappears – each drop
a story of the formless in search
of a travel line.

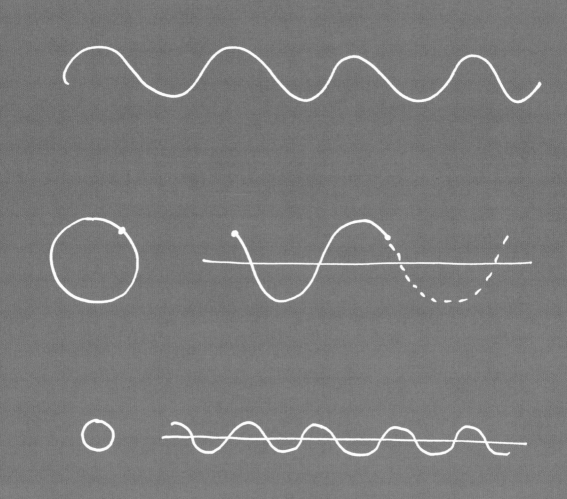

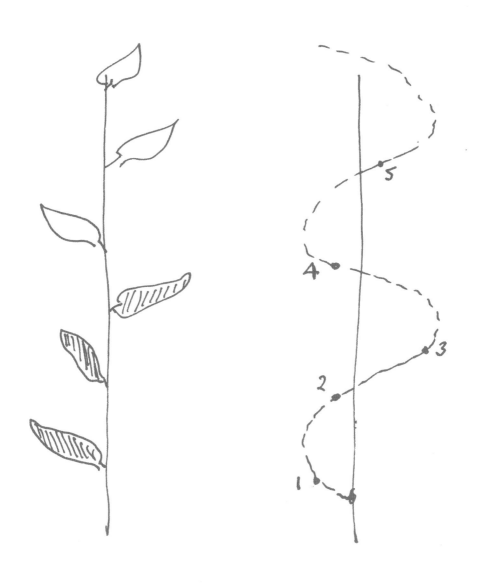

E nergy too is a wave. But the wave has a signature, its form generated by the dot moving around a circle. The path taken around the circumference translates into an undulating line. The wave travels. So does the plant – its axis vertical. To grow there has to be an open-ended element, an asymmetry within a symmetry; and the plant tracks a helix in its search for light, compacting and optimising. Leaves rotate about the vertical at a special angle such that maximum light is allowed through to what is below. In the angles turned about the stem a particular ratio hides called a 'golden' ratio. From a set of numbers called the 'Fibonacci' sequence this value arises, a unique property where there needs to be a measure of control and growth, repeated at different scales. Nature likes such a strategy, and not surprisingly fractals also have the same controlling characteristic, beneath their cascades of self-similar patterning.

The plant criss-crosses a circle in its search for light.

The best angle between successive leaf growth is 137.5 degrees.
Then 222.5 degrees completes the circle – the larger value divided
by the smaller produces the golden ratio, approximately 1.618
– spiral forms arise from such patterning.

The Fibonacci sequence.
Adding two previous numbers to get the next, the series grows in controlled jumps. There has to be a start, so it is 1. Add the unit to its predecessor, which is zero, and the second value becomes 1 again. The next number is 2, made up by adding 1 and 1. Then 2 and 1 makes 3, and so on. Going back to go forward is a conservation, controlling excess. Higher adjacent values of the sequence, when divided one by the other, produce the golden ratio.

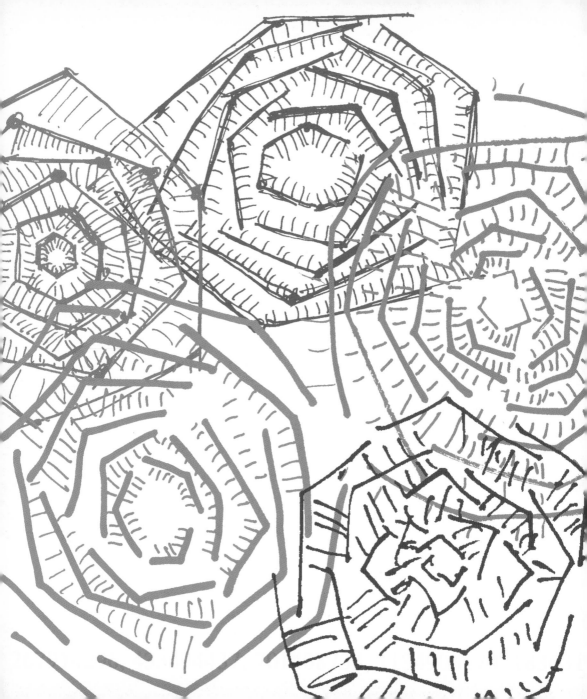

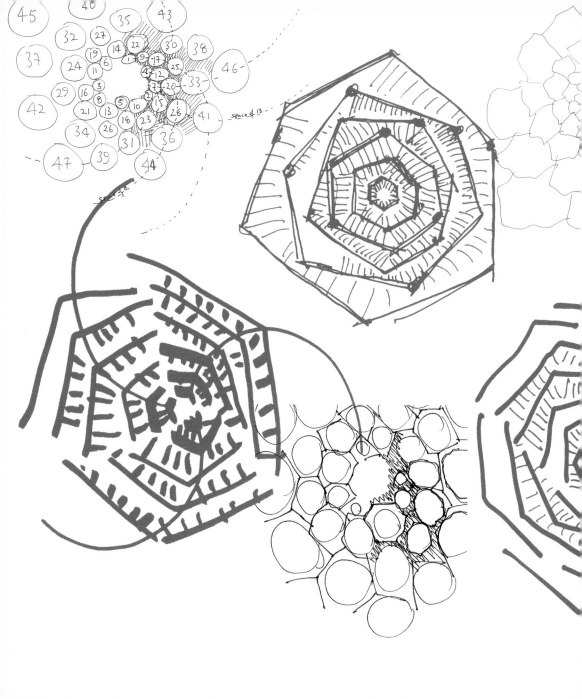

space of 13

space of 8

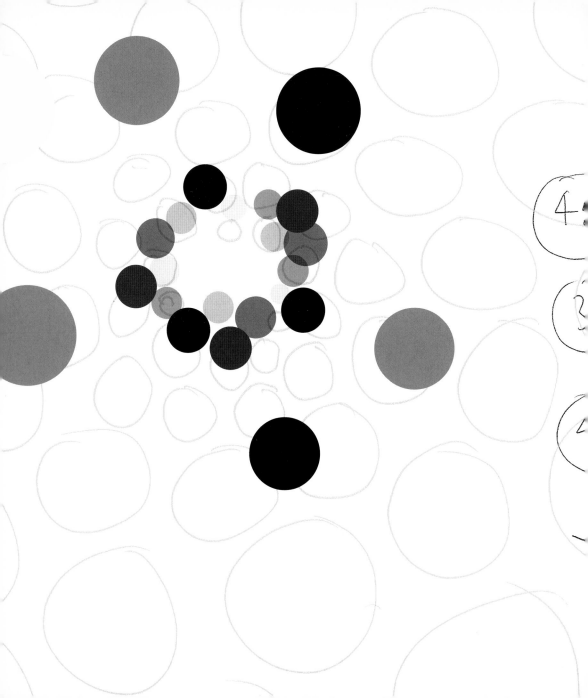

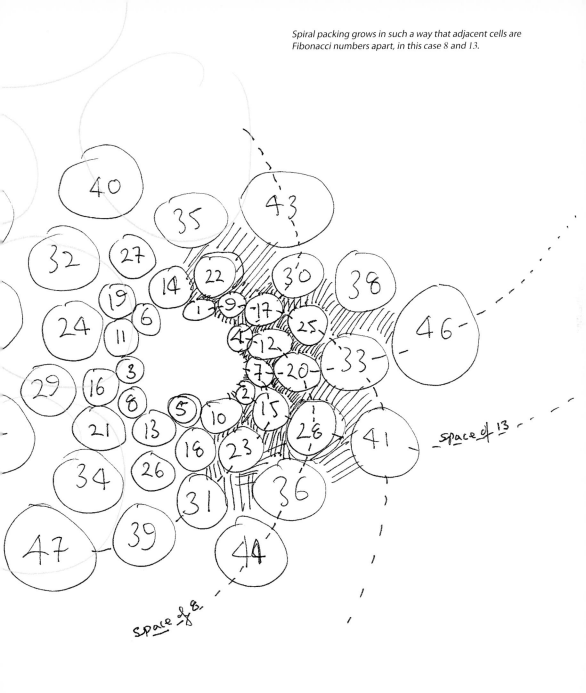

Spiral packing grows in such a way that adjacent cells are Fibonacci numbers apart, in this case 8 and 13.

space of 13

space of 8.

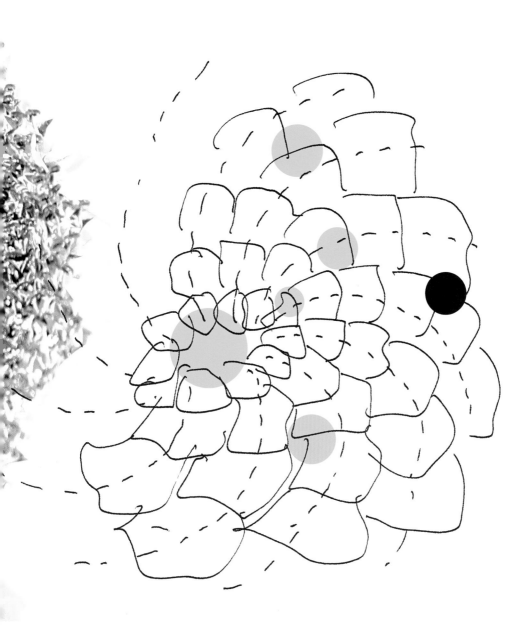

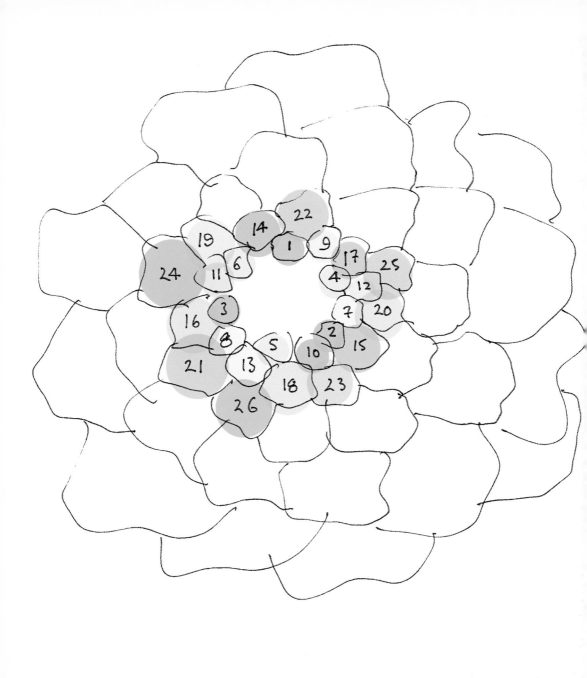

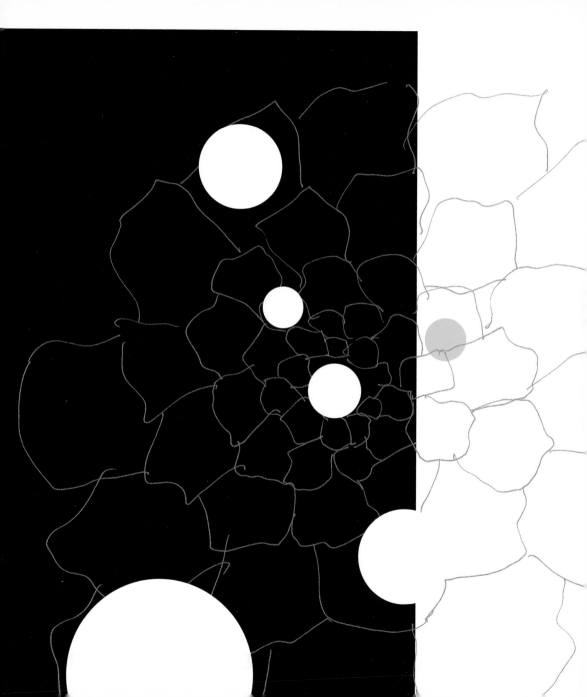

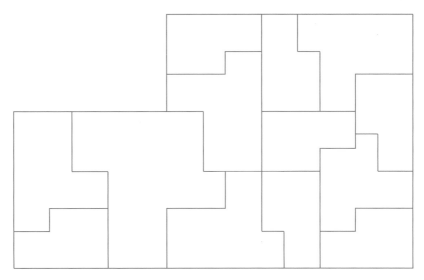

The golden section occurs in mathematical mosaics – or 'tiling' – that are packed together tightly to produce beautiful mappings in space.

A puzzle unfolds with *aperiodic* tiling. Like a jigsaw, different shapes interlock to produce a picture but the detail here is one that changes throughout. No part of it can be cut out and moved along to match, identically, another. There is always a misfit. The pattern is non-translatable. But it's not chaotic and varying continuously, there is a control that inhibits excess: only a few shapes are needed to make the fit hold. The tiles have a particular facility, within each is embedded not only smaller and similar shapes of itself but to the same reduced scale the other shapes also interlock. Each tile is a hybrid. This way a sequence grows like branching, each tile reproducing smaller versions of a bigger picture. What gives the pattern special powers is the controlling hand again of the particular value of the 'golden' ratio – it surfaces in the dimensions of the tiles and their fit along a series of shifting orthogonal grids. The rectangles formed by the intersection of these hidden grids, at all scales, have proportions which are also 'golden'.

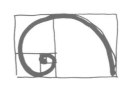 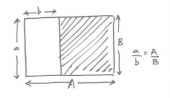

A rectangle is 'golden' if a square taken away from it leaves behind a rectangle that has the same length to breadth proportion as the original. Repeating this idea leads to the logarithmic spiral, the signature underlying natural growth.

$$\frac{a}{b} = \frac{A}{B}$$

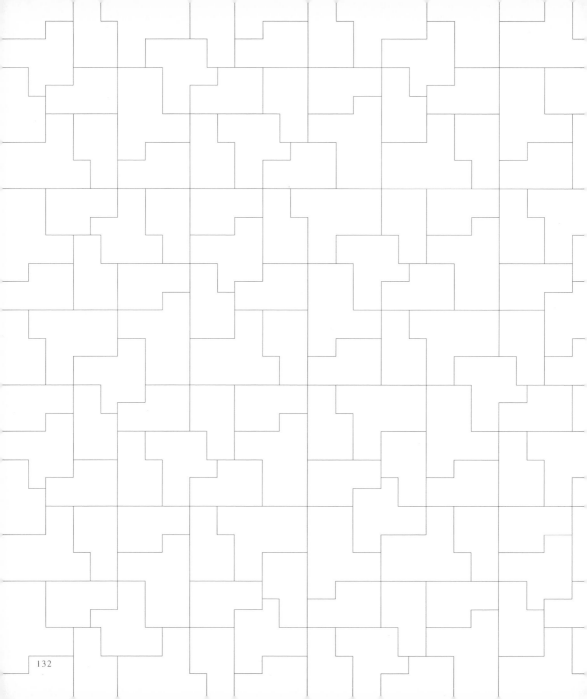

132

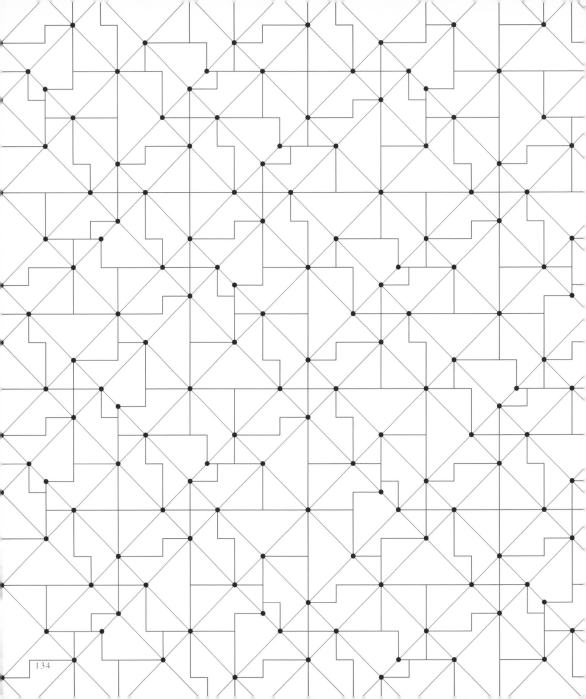

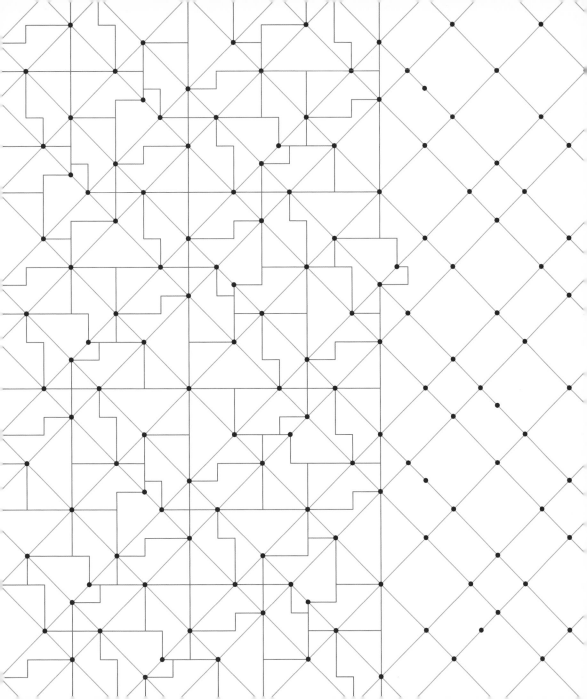

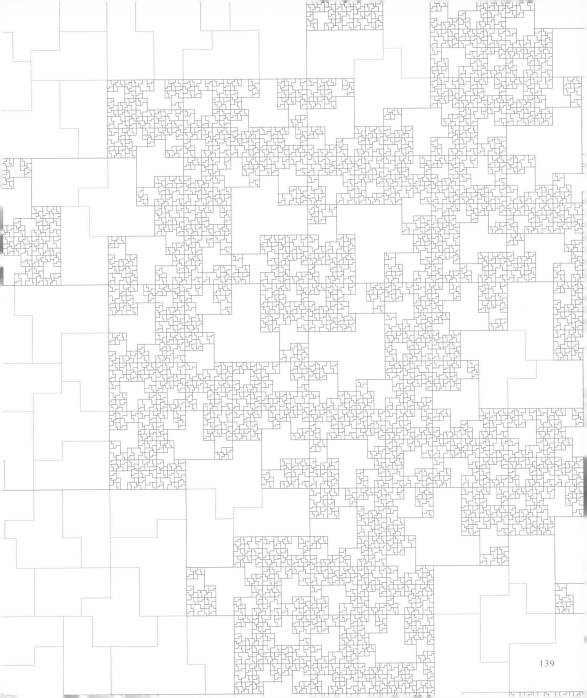

139

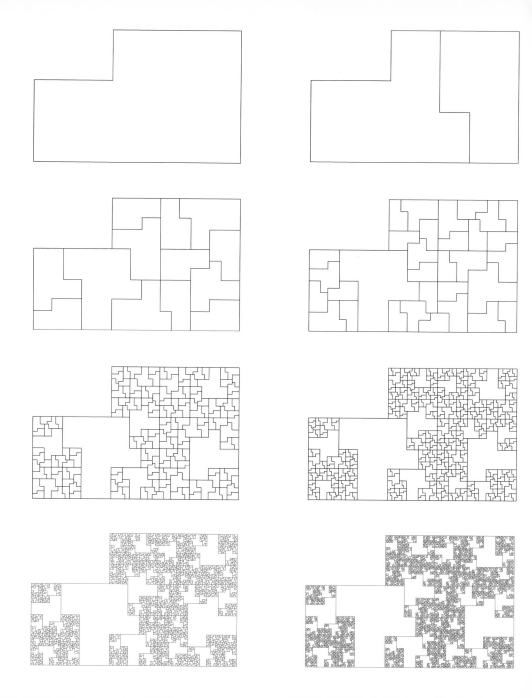

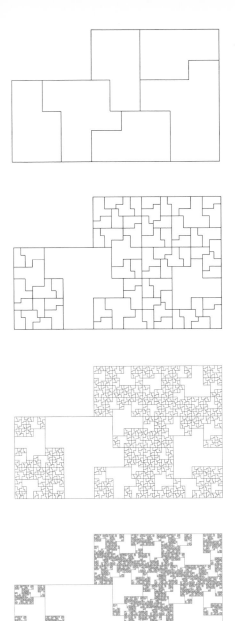

At each scale down, as one shape is stopped 'holes' appear in the pattern and a tiling grows – what looks like a subdivision is really a branching, like a tree gets ever finer towards its canopy. Here the 'canopy' is thickest where the most dense and minutest folding occurs, where diagonal lines appear in the patterns. The tiling is fractal.

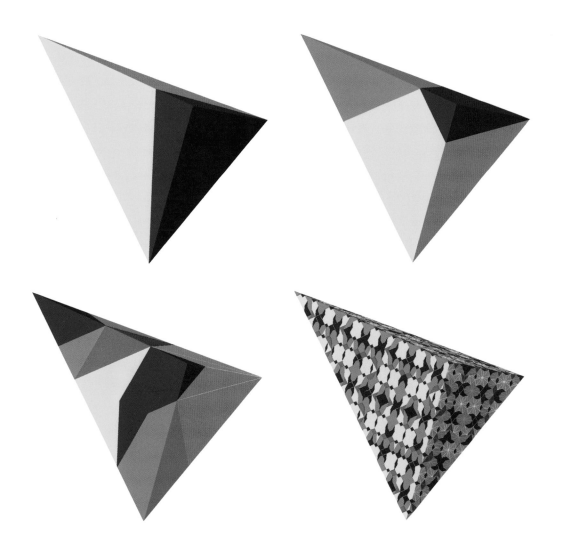

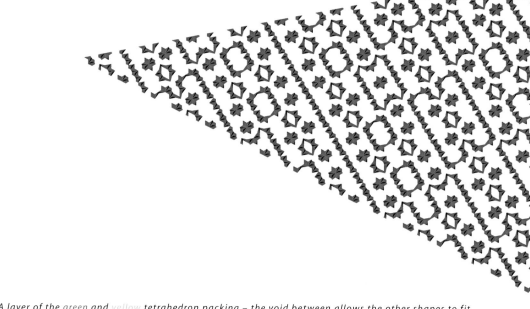

A layer of the green and yellow tetrahedron packing – the void between allows the other shapes to fit.

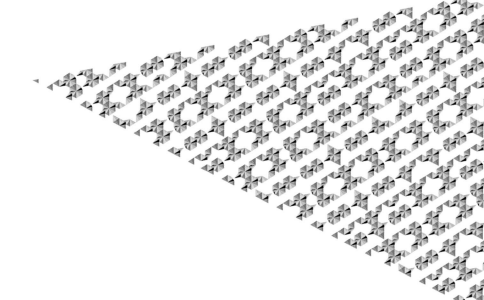

Where three tiles produced aperiodic tiling in two dimensions, three dimensional tiling, or now 'packing', needs four separate shapes. They are tetrahedral. Each shape can be made up by smaller versions of itself and the other tiles. Jigsaw within a jigsaw. The intricate packing of space produced is called 'Danzer'. (The basic 3D structure of rocks and minerals is the tetrahedron.)

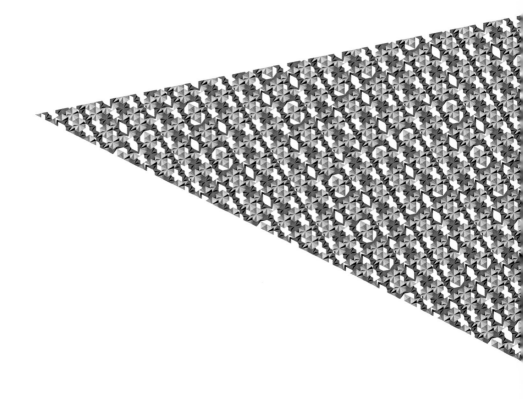

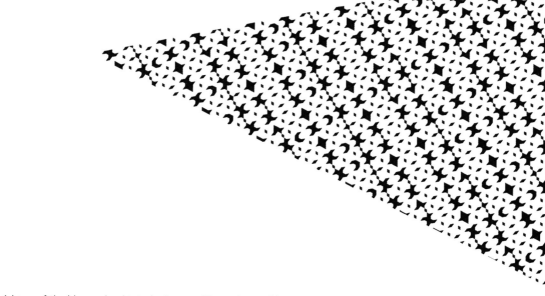

A layer of the blue and *red* tetrahedron packing – the void between allows the other shapes to fit.

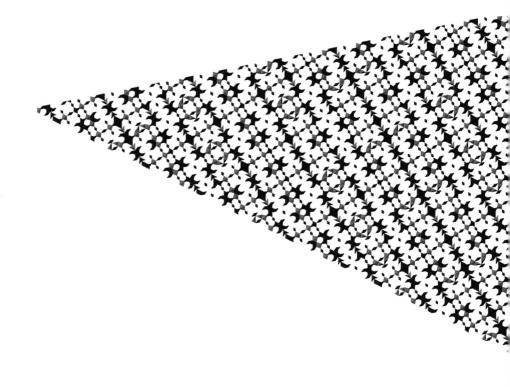

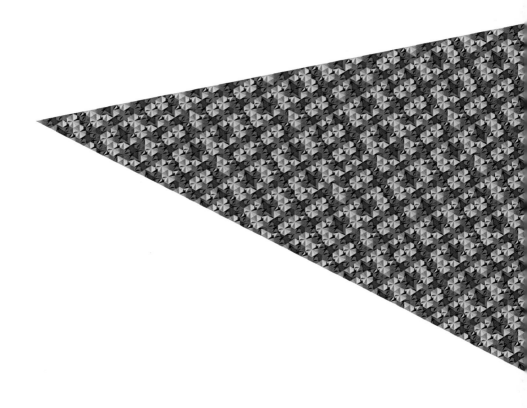

*The pattern is infinite in its depth, a series of complex forms;
we travel forever down its many-fold symmetries.*

But against my own body Nature looms large: the diversity endless, full of invention, impossible to chart.

Like a tangled knot defies analysis, too much is going on in bush and plant and variety of species. But in the build up of the clouds to thunder, the weather following the ocean currents, the growing delta of the river mouth

– in the constant building and demolition and rebuilding – I find Nature an artisan, working away on a mission impossible. The hewing, forging, harvesting, and the seasons' turn is tireless. If I engage with this construct then only do I see the patterns – ridges, hollows, coastlines and continents, leaves branching in networks, tree bark in wave forms. The markings are everywhere. Nothing is without this strategy. And in the muscles and bones (of the making of the thing) I find an animation – beauty. The fright at the External slows down. In the small steps of close observation I ask what is the proposal of changing proportion or shifting colour that makes this or that beautiful? Even in the terrors of the storm or violent cascades I see pattern – shockingly, it may be beautiful. Beauty is a construct beyond morality.

The design may be seen as on a circle, the different characters and forms to Nature.

Around one half is the physical:

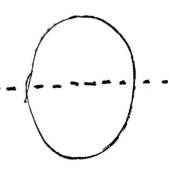

The first thought is of something immense, huge, out there outside of my skin; the impression of Nature as a Surrounding that stretches far and wide. And encompassing everything. I walk, run, swim and journey in its immersion; even at home that outside keeps humming. I am aware of the dimension that wraps all. I breathe it in. I cannot escape – I must be part of it. But that continuous awareness comes only later, after I travel around the circle, stopping at each stage and engaging with each form.

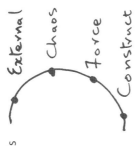

External
Chaos
Force
Construct

On the other half are the abstracts we gain from the above:

Interior
Order
Beauty
Pattern

If the right side is body, the left creates the animation behind what we see, call it spirit. The circle balances body with spirit – invisible connections cross the void – an intricate stitching rather than the simple counterbalance of a seesaw.

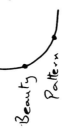

External

The External shoots out in a bolt to the stars. Along the way the warp of gravity bends and tangles it all up – and the stitching of the cosmos takes over. In starpoint a galaxy bigger than ours, a super-giant, sucks in the thread and sends it farther to more distant globular clusters, and the primal areas of what might be next out of the void. The distance keeps jumping and stretching. Each stretch a quantum of scale. In the end, not that there is really an end, we stop counting; the zeros of distance are uncontrollable. There is no limit – just more scattering of dots around an endless loop, finite but unbounded. Some think, within the dots are the shadows of other universes. Big and uncountable as our domain is, there may be a whole sea of universes that we ride, and us just one small speck in a much bigger picture.

To every leap in scale travelled out there is a corresponding shrink to a dimension travelled within. From cover of skin, inwards to muscle tissue, veins, protein chains, blood molecules and DNA coiling, and then crossing the threshold into the sub-atomic world, space seems to proportion itself so that the void within is as layered as the void outside. Beneath the atomic structure are sub-particles; then the quarks and, at last, just vibrations – as the physicists say, 'superstrings'. (Are we like a conduit, allowing superstring to megastring pass through, and does not our mind create the argument in the first place?)

But I feel alone and outside these things stranded within myself. Nature is wild and infinite: the woodland, the valley side and the river runs, my footfall on scrub and weed, and grass beyond measure; I am the dot – the mere speck that travels through these domains. I am a sieve for all these pathways to slip through, how else do I feel connected? When I look up at the stars at night or melt a drop of dew on my finger the largest and the smallest takes my mind in jumps, unsure of scale, I fix on the pattern, and shrink or expand in its force.

A merry-go-round! Nature's fair is for excitement and discovery – the stalls a chatter of confusion, but also a delight and a pleasure.

The croton leaf stipples colours, the orchid dots and streaks; the leopard has her spots, the tiger his stripes. Rhododendrons, poinsettias, fox-gloves, daisies, chrysanthemums, palm trees, oaks, silver birch, elm, punctuate and multiply the variations. And lichen on mountains, heather on moors, creepers in the jungle, fungi in the earth – the pickings are rich. If we take the 'big dipper' we would climb into the airy regions and see clouds charge up into fantastic formations, massive tornados churning within dark atmospheres, then plunge into the ocean to view currents and whirlpools and the river's cataract flood. In special areas drift the sand dunes, their ridges like serpents; in these basins of desert, circular winds draw breathtaking stories. In the wet realm signs warn 'Keep Out!' around quicksands and sucking bogs: in fissures beyond, the geysers shoot out from the earth in pillars of scalding water. My mind goes numb with the sights but some memories stay. The more I think upon it, certain features repeat.

Only a few outlines make up leaves; a certain way do petals grow around their stem. Self-similar waves pattern the tree bark, or rock. It is as if out of a few basic elements and props that the stalls and arcades of the variety show are built. The shapes – tendrilled, bobbed, jagged, flared, also carry identifying marks. From tiniest dot to broadest stripe, and in-between zigzags, specks or striations, each mark has patterns if one looks closer, with similar strategies often to the form that bears them. One echoes the other. Does not a leaf up close, look like its distant tree?

A shape is made by wave forms, energy subjected to the surrounding environment. The same is true of how the mark is made on a shape. For the concentrations are local that give bias and begin a process. Colour is fed on pigment and densities, porosities, refraction indices. There are viscosities, flows that yield gradients, electrical charges which form the substrates that trigger reactions; local actions of frequency, pH value, nutrients, form the object or shape. No surprise then that there are self-similarities.

To reach the widest sample the beginnings have to be simple, and the smallest. The more elaborate the start the fewer the options to grow into. Imagine a connected structure and develop it – the possible shapes are limited right from the start by the existing connections which get in the way. Even a line is a limitation; but shrink to a dot and in potential the infinite becomes possible. If I look with x-ray eyes into the so-called chaos, root motifs are revealed, a few geometric ideas that by stretching, diluting, mixing, overlapping and so on forge a wide interest. Micro-actions govern. Where a pigmentation begins or shape ends, the local idea sets a tendency that then feeds back into the process, growing or repeating, augmenting or diminishing. Underneath the destination as it were are the births of many possible journeys. What we see are not the answers – there is always more to come, to experiment with.

The Tsunami skinned a woman, a five-hundred-kilometre-per-hour wave gathered grit from the ocean bed and in tiny granules scrubbed the skin off her hand and leg as the sea swept into a fishing village. Somewhere else lightning split a tree in half; and on the slopes of a mountain the ground opened to swallow a settlement whole, the earthquake tearing up a fault line.

Nature is voracious. Tornados suck people and homes into their eye, walls of water in the sea drown shipping. The disasters are named back to the Great Flood and beyond, angry gods that rage and strike in fury. Zeus setting off thunderbolts; Poseidon bringing up serpents from the deep; not just one god but many to cope with the faces of fear. And the wildness is brought closer in the presence of a figure to bow to: Shango – god of thunder; Agni – god of fire; Durga – god of early death, with her belt of infant skulls around her waist. Different names, Behemoth, Ashtar, Indu, Aphrodite, Kuveni, Boab, Enskil... the people change, but the forces persist. Lightning/Flood/Famine/Storm, the demons still have to be appeased.

Spirits hide in everything, trees, rivers, streams, in stones by the wayside. The forests and pathways come alive with forces that have to be talked to, most importantly connected to, by repeating cadences of dance or words. Pattern itself becomes a force.

The votive offerings go up and touch the planets: Mars as god of war, Venus as star of Beauty. Force not just destructive but also benign. The abstractions began early: the Sun combined such powers, to raise the dawn from the clutch of night and give life or parch the day to shrivel and

burns at the core of the sun fusing hydrogen to heavier helium; once the chain begins other atoms form. The Elements emerge. One by one a serial count of atomic number grows from hydrogen 1 to uranium 92. The sequence is found scattered in the sun and stars; and we in turn are samples of such counts in wild space. The elements are the ingredients of a universal soup. As the sun ages it will implode, the gas cloud thrown into space will seethe with the stuff of this world; from the debris another sun will fire up. On cosmic scales each flare adds seed material. Without being aware of the violent flames trapped within, we harbour the inventions of such stardust – and the universe.

But the fears continue, the forces do not go away. Today in temples, mosques and churches, prayers and chants appease the powers that they may be contained, and not released, now in nuclear blast or by a virus let loose on a fragile ecology.

die – the Sun measured good and evil. 'Let there be light' was the command in Genesis; before that was only the chilling darkness. So intimate with our being, this Phenomenon shoots its photons packed with energy to turn the chlorophyll of plants to oxygen, which foments life.

But there is a family of powers at work. The forces of nature that bind the world come in four degrees, gravity – the weakest, then electromagnetism or the charge between particles, and then two nuclear forces, one weak, one strong. The strongest force

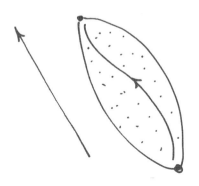

Force is path of least resistance between two potentials

Easy to see that Nature is a construct – mountains climb their sides in ridges and zigzag lines, valleys dip and run or lie flat in broad swathes. Waves pile up and unfurl. Look at the sky to watch the wind work on trees and clouds. Out of the air fire sucks on its combustion.

The Construct may be seen in four parts – Earth, Air, Fire, Water – one solid, the others liquid, combustive or vaporous. Early philosophers saw it as arranged in a square on its end, as in a diamond, Earth lying opposite Air, and Fire in opposition to Water. Earth is the element of hard substance; the other parts, formless. To travel round the square is to find Earth covered by Water, which in turn is covered by Air. After that comes the realm of Fire or the ascent of energy, and from that creative in all things the Earth and its minerals are born. Between Earth and Water is a sub-agenda, cold; between Water and Air, wet. Air and Fire are said to have the quality of heat between them; and between Fire and Earth, dryness. The dynamic is that fire is hot and dry, earth dry and cold, and so on. The elements cycle.

and draw fault lines. Lava spills. Molten currents are trapped in flow paths in the rock face. As tectonic plates driven by the plasmic tide crush into each other mountains form, the length of the contact raising the Alps, the Andes, the Himalayas. Even steam is part of a construct, hissing out of the fractures only to join the vapours and fall back down as rain. Rain falls into the rivers that run into the ocean, the rivers wash away the earth and silt and sediment. Again the deposits that settle are marked by the flow and eddying of those saturating currents. Just as in the hollow chambers of the sky moisture turns to rain, in deep space unseen clouds of gas cluster, condense, and erupt in great cosmic flares as supernovae. Out of the explosions come stars and planets – the earth, and the atmosphere, and rain. The elements cycle.

But the act of construction has only a few opportunities, either to branch, fold, or pack. Trees branch, brains fold. Earth is packed, so is water. Lightning branches, so does fire. Mountains fold. In the sub-regions of the atom another construct must be added, that of knotting; or the interweave of energy packets in electrons and quantum strings or loops. (A knot is the generic, for it can be seen to branch and fold and pack at the same time.)

If once we saw the four elements as Earth, Air, Fire and Water, today the picture would be not

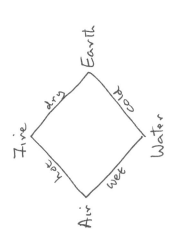

At the heart of the Earth is a solid core, floating and rotating, surrounded by molten material still plasmic, cindering and burning from its origin. On the tides of these gigantic oceans floats the cooling mantle in several pieces, sometimes loosely joined, from half to many kilometres thick. When chunks of it fall off into the miasma below the crust shudders and splits in spasm. Earthquakes accelerating through rock and alluvium layers release fractures, of the classification and its objects but of the construct that stirs behind them. To branch, fold, pack or knot, is to look into Nature's mindset as a community of actions. Be they solid, vaporous or incendiary, the few instructions to make Order! compile the panoramas. The wonderful outcome is a licence to exist, but in only a few ways. The whole is irreducible – that is the challenge of the new order.

We move across. Slip around the circle.

Dot and dash make the connections – stars join up to form the animals of the zodiac, water holes reduce to circles, snakes become zigzags and mountains draw as triangles – we look to make codes. Make it simple, easier to spread the mind that way, and move faster towards the interior. As we rush at the landscape we mark, in shorthand, pictures in our mind that overlay the site of the actual image. We play. Clouds move as dashed lines and fleeting dots, reedbeds turn to vertical strokes over horizontal rows of bubbles; the tree in code is the same as for the delta of a river. Water is an up-and-down mark, the wave figure. The first step towards the interior is pattern.

metaphor ← PATTERN → Concrete

Before counting, noting down patterns was an act of survival: maps had to be made to remember locations of poison or predators. In the cycle of plants and weather, even time grew a pattern. To repeat is important – safety lies that way. (A constant varying without stop would be an impossible headache to contain; with no meaning given to the noise and scatter.) So the first step to civilise is to find order, to pattern. Forty thousand years ago a cave dweller marked a set of lines crossing each other on the side of a small rock; diagonal to right and horizontal, diagonal to left, drawing as a result a pattern of diamonds. What he or she was describing is unknown, but the desire to code and abstract and then improvise held fast. Millennia later, geometry developed, and mathematics. We grew to make shapes that only the mind's eye wants to see. With music and the rhythms of a poem, we unlock even larger emotional pictures, fleshed out by the beats in our head.

If our senses act it is in the notation of patterns. And these patterns link the metaphors we conceive to the realities we make. A set of wavy lines could serve as the grain in wood or act for the idea of 'flexible'. Gas molecules may be dots, also star clusters, and dots may serve as 'scatter'. Metaphors instigate creative acts, which end in the fact of an object or event. Observing that fact will raise a pattern in our heads, which in turn leads back to metaphor. Back and forth the game is played: from the concrete to the abstract, the bridge between being pattern. The diagram shorthand keeps breathing life into our minds as a subversive act. We seem to be wired this way.

The pattern behind pattern, beauty is mysterious, and hard to pin down. A force in nature's interior, beauty moves on hidden planes, away from the physical fact and the literal towards an inward magnification. Something awakens a secret x-factor that plays with balance, varying tensions, and pulls the mind one way. Colours, sounds, the steps of a dance suddenly create harmonies that lift our spirits – we are happy to be alive.

To engage with this secret seems to be necessary, not just with a prettiness but with the argument of a complex mix; small parts of awkwardness along with the smoothness of symmetry – confluences that power the work, proportions and textures and gradients that gather swiftly into silent unstoppable song – so that we say 'beautiful'. Something to do with the way things are made – seeing that they have been wrought by sweat and imagination, the difficulties made effortless ultimately. Not just an object but a body of delight; not just a lake mirroring the sky – or a sunset – but a joy stretched amongst our senses.

Beauty lies in the struggle of mists to wrap the valley sides, or in terrain swept by winds and etched in lines of rains and storm. It seems to be in the action of water as it froths over rapids and shakes itself to find quieter pools, and in the swift work of clouds moving from one outline to another.

Coastlines, mountains grained and bent by larval flow make landscapes a shaping art, forged by time. The scale down from trunk to stem, leaf to bud, in tracery of tree against the sky, the rhythm of forest delights in different stages of branchings. Over tumbling boulders and sliding ranges the valleys slope from high to low, in cascades. Nothing

seems fixed. Even water and sheet ice fluctuate as the mood of light and atmosphere take hold. To see time in features is to witness change.

The imprint of a process and its rates of change mark our own private radar. We pattern an aesthetic sense, for refinement, delicate balance, trial and error. Sometimes what is beautiful sours, and we lose an appetite for it. But the pattern behind beauty is poetic and outlives fashion – a compulsive will that forces us to invent and abstract. Its essence borders on intoxication. When the patterns or poems we reach place tremors upon us, we call that sublime, something ineffable joins us to the core of nature. A deep drum calls, a heart beat that dares us to reach forward. There is no moralising here, no placements of good or evil, but a plain hunger to evolve.

Use repeatedly a few building blocks: bind together the nucleus of an atom with proton and neutron, and orbit electrons around that centre balancing their negative charge against the positives of the protons. Then start counting with hydrogen atomic number 1 (the unit is for the number of protons) and up the Periodic Table to heavier elements. Oxygen counts 8, neon is 10, uranium 92. A simple act, the success of hydrogen, is built upon and a series grows – the elements, up to 92 of them. Everything in and under the sun is embedded with them. Carbon makes diamonds and charcoal. Sodium and Chloride make salt. Carbon bonds with Hydrogen to build organic molecules like proteins, blood, and us.

Electrons form shells around the nucleus whizzing in and out. When eight electrons fill one shell, another grows. The heaviest atom has fourteen 'clouds' of electrons roaming round its centre. Like arms outstretched, the valencies of one atom reach for another. The element that has a few electrons in a shell jumps at the opportunity to borrow from another, to complete its shells and form a compound substance. Sodium is volatile this way and likes to mix readily. Argon is not; its outer shells are full, it is viewed as 'inert'. And so on... The elements and their compounds arise from a few entities with set patterns for bonding among them.

At a macro level, at the scale of many billions times that of an atom, the plant or flower also shows consistent ways of growing by, at the same time, adding and jumping. In controlled steps the petal growth in flowers is counted as 3 for lilies and irises, 5 for buttercups, 8 for some delphiniums, 13 for marigolds, 21 for asters, and 34, 55 and 89 is the count for the daisies. Such

Fibonacci sequence... 13, 21, 34, 55. (like 55/34) to approximate to the value of φ – the joints of our fingers arise in such a fixed ratio. And our overall height in relation to the distance our navel is from the ground approximates towards the same measure. It seems to be everywhere, where natural growth occurs. (Similarly, in the long to short diameter of an egg – and the spans of the butterfly, its wing-tip breadth to body length – the same ratio. And so on....)

The golden ratio is a trigger for a system to have maximum success.

When a system is inert, a fix of proportions and placements, it stays that way. But if the system is dynamic there has to be the ability to exchange information all the time. At all scales data is fed through and transformed. To do this easily is to succeed at a small scale, and then add to each part the same geometry, adding and growing, feeding back the idea each time. What begins as a small set of instructions is multiplied into a complex web, self-similar at all measures.

There is no uncontrolled growth here pushing to excess; instead a measured rule, cycling obediently.

A kaleidoscope of form in nature is released this way. What seems many on the outside is counted carefully, internally, in steady doses of structure and growth. As the plant matures, leaves around the stem rotate and climb to catch the sun with least interference to what lies below. (The opportunity is marked by a spacing related to a special ratio.) Each leaf bears a constant arc to the previous one – like on a snail's shell, each revolution is proportioned by a controlled jump. This jump around a plant stem is about 137.5° – that leaves 222.5° to complete a full rotation of 360°. And 222.5/137.5 approximates to 1.618, denoted by the Greek letter φ (Phi) called the 'golden ratio'. One way to discover the value is to divide successive higher numbers of the

numbers also order the rotation of cross spirals in the way an acorn grows or the sunflower spreads its centre. The same numbers are in the arrangement of the cells of a pineapple skin. These numbers are called the Fibonacci numbers. They annotate the study of Phyllotaxis (plant and leaf growth) and arise as a sequence by adding the two previous values of a particular series to produce the next number. One step back to go forward.

1 1 2 3 5 8 13 21

Co-existing one within the other, with similar patterns, is the sign of a fractal. The branches in our lungs to exchange oxygen, the bundling of the clouds to exchange moisture, the winding in and out of the coastlines to exchange land with the sea, are all imprints of fractal organisations. Seen this way, the fractal is a massive filter between two mediums.

But beneath intricate fold and delicate branch, the history of the event cannot be unwound to reveal the original idea; like a human cannot be tracked back to the exact cell he or she was conceived from. The complexity is locked in. We are non-linear creatures. The cells can only be followed from the moment of conception, to the foetus, and then to later infant. We cannot unwind.

Nothing is solid in the interior. This region is not like a cave or a closed volume but open, unbounded and ever-expanding. Each external object is sucked into its domain and inverts to a fiction; the fiction is far greater than the scope of the fact. The Interior is an area of potential, a place of becoming. Nothing is without that is not within. In this circular statement our skins are pricked as we join patterns with the universe.

My mind in its fevers conjures seas of meditations or cliffs of anguish, developing metaphors from the landscape that surrounds. What is heard, seen and touched is transposed quickly from the surrounding fact to the imagination. Is Nature really physical, of flesh and blood, concrete and solid? Yes, we say – it's common sense – but it takes only an instant to go beyond the literal, passing beyond colour and shape to reach the intangible of an 'immediacy'. It seems impossible to 'look' without being aware that there are hidden measures which identify with us. When we immerse ourselves in Nature's habitat we feel we receive answers, our senses unravel to allow something already part of us to join forces.

If Nature imagined itself, would it have our senses? Tears and laughter? Would its own touch soothe and calm? Is the nature of our imagination the patterned reflection of nature's own structures?

And there are tricks to contend with; continuous touch undermines the very sense it projects, just as prolonged staring blinds. Press one's hand on a rock. The hard fact soon disappears; and emotion, memory, combine to make a new construction. The longer my hand stays against the hard surface the more I pass through the stone, as if its matrix hardness were nothing, the formless so quick to eat up the certainty. Similarly, if I dip my hand in a river stream the cold water burns my fingers and wrist to a steel hardness, the water is solid hot to the touch. From water to stone the journey is limited only by my imagination.

Reality seems to be in the running mind that has no limit, endless in its metaphors and inventions. When the keys we use are buried deep in our mind, what is the real, and physical? The busiest place to be on the circle is the Interior, a fantastic point of all possibilities. The form to be, the dreams that may chance structure, is in this crucible of the virtual.

And from Interior we move to the Exterior, but to realise another fact of the world. The outcome will bring with it the nightmares that accompany certainty, was it well done, or is it fit? Has the event lost so much of what may have been achieved? Subversive questions – it pushes us back to think, imagine and create again. Nature does the same, its additions, subtractions, multiplications refining and honing, compelled always to make again. That leap from the possible to the real is a constant trial.

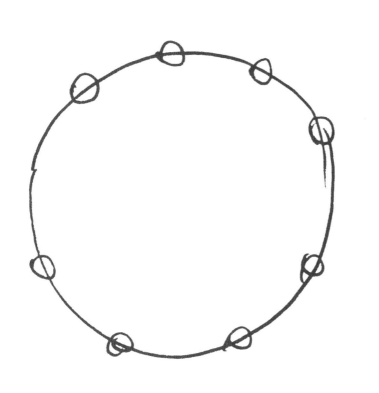

Move now to point one of the circle and begin again.

Move from meditation to material and join External, Chaos, Force, Construct – facts of the body – to Pattern, Beauty, Order, Interior – thoughts on Spirit. Through both, creation circles.

As we gaze into the world and look up at the stars and gauge their meanings, we draw a blanket around us and huddle up under the darkness, to play the games of children — secret house, all the more appealing than rushing at the world outside. In the darknesses our mind floats free. Blinded we see more, imagine greater. The facts dissolve. The world within, haunted by the after-image of the outside, fragments, blurs; and we create new worlds out of the virtual. The nurturing of phantoms is more exciting, the word for that is also Pattern. What is in Spirit soon becomes Body. Nature seems not to be a trick but a spontaneous mirror held up to ourselves. I go behind my eyes and close them, pull down the shutters, and look within.

The Element takes hold, the cycle begins.

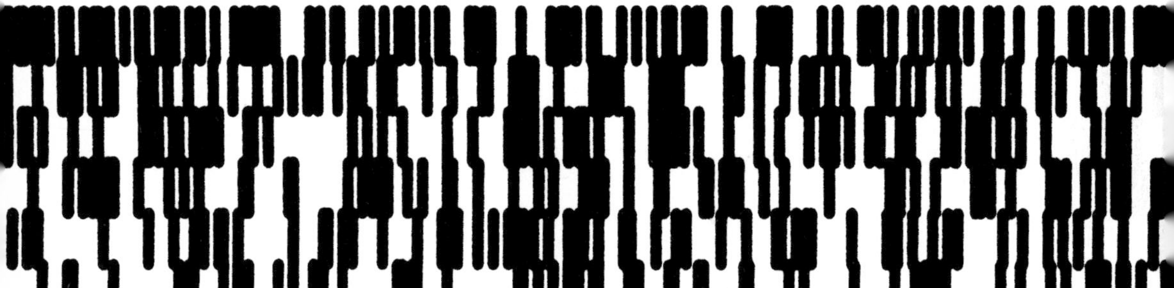

Un-colonised, un-aggregated, non-composite, prime numbers stand alone. Like the root underlying a many branching, prime is an essential quality. Without it there would be no structure. From the simple and the singular to the many and the complex, prime is the blueprint for growth in a world of numbers. Primes are thoroughly informal – they shift, jump, to no regular order – there is no exact location. But once found, we can follow the trail back and track the steps. Looking at the actual value is not that interesting but plotting the gaps, in how the primes move forward, is illuminating. There seems to be an order – we feel there are repeat patterns – yet one cannot be found. At the heart of our arithmetic is a flow of uncertainty.

Gaps between prime numbers plotted relative to each other as rising or falling steps.

An even number is made up of two prime numbers in many ways – such as 32 is the sum of 1 and 31 or 3 and 29 or 13 and 19. As such combinations are plotted vertically against an axis of the even numbers horizontally, a beautiful shifting pattern grows, as if a breeze riffles through the foliage of the number elements. Zooming in and blowing up a part shows the serial rhythm hidden in the primes.

The March of Primes starting with 1, growing past 3, 5, 7, 11... climbing higher, 29, 31... past 101, 103, 109... and higher and farther... 271, 277, 281... into the thousands and beyond, the sentinels of number theory climb. Primes are atomic substance, of numbers. They cannot be factored. Divided only by themselves or by 1, primes are inviolate. Other numbers have chameleon-like natures. What is the multiplicity of thirty? 3x10 or 15x2 or 5x6? But 30 can be factored down into 2x3x5 and whichever way the factorising is done only these numbers will be reached ultimately, none other. The root multipliers are all prime.

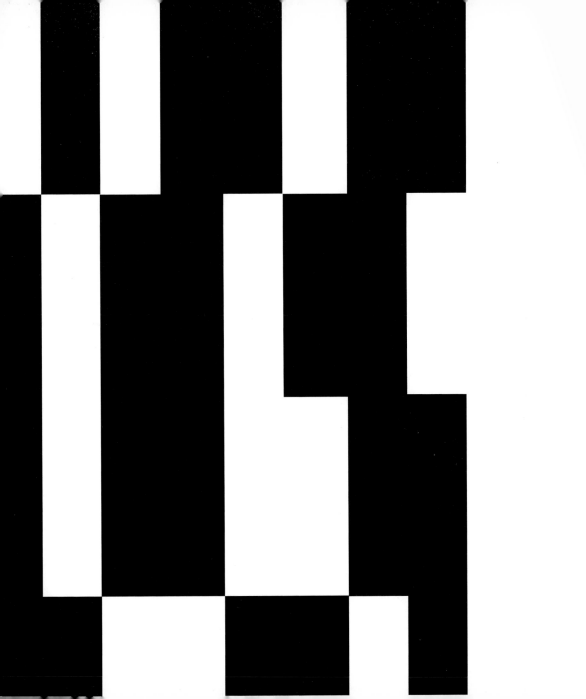

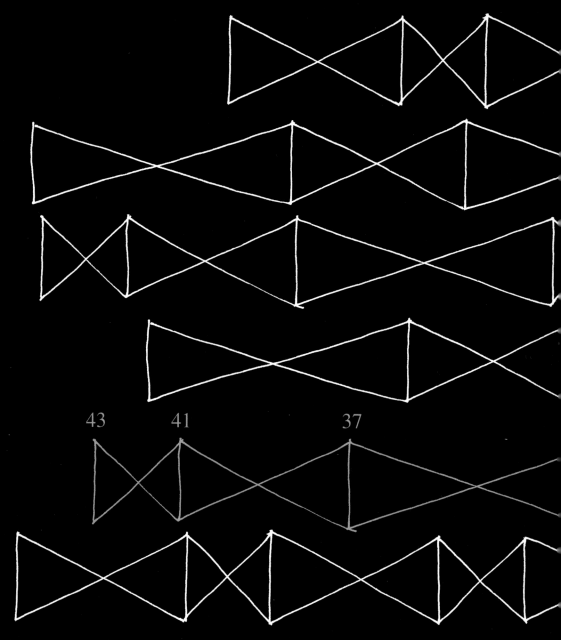

43   41   37

Gaps between primes shown as Brancusi diamonds.

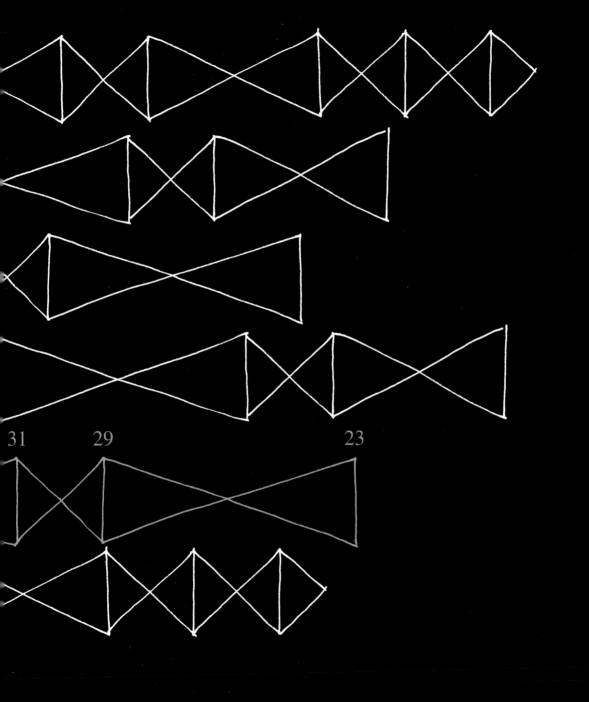

31   29   23

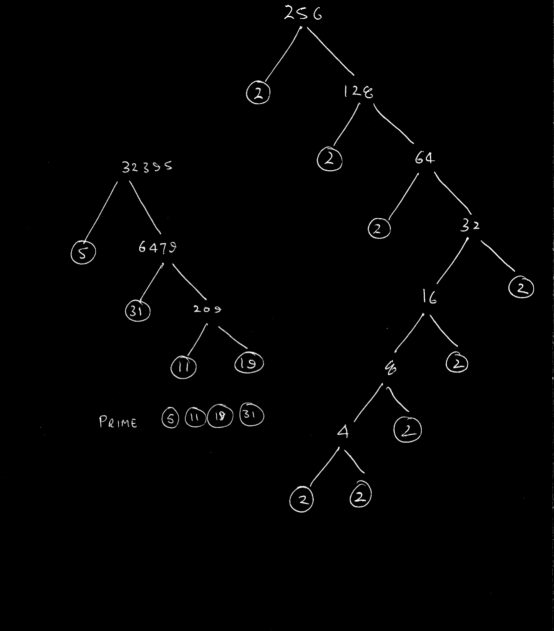

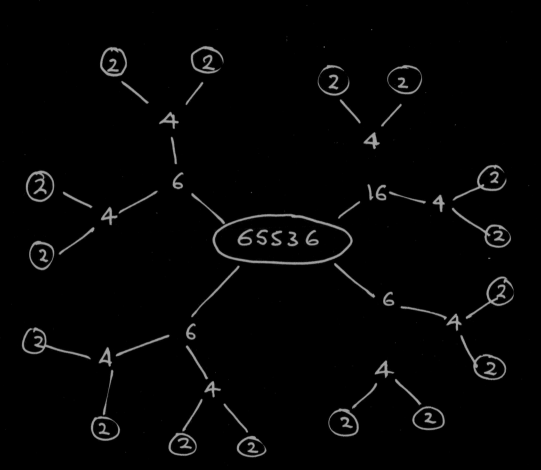

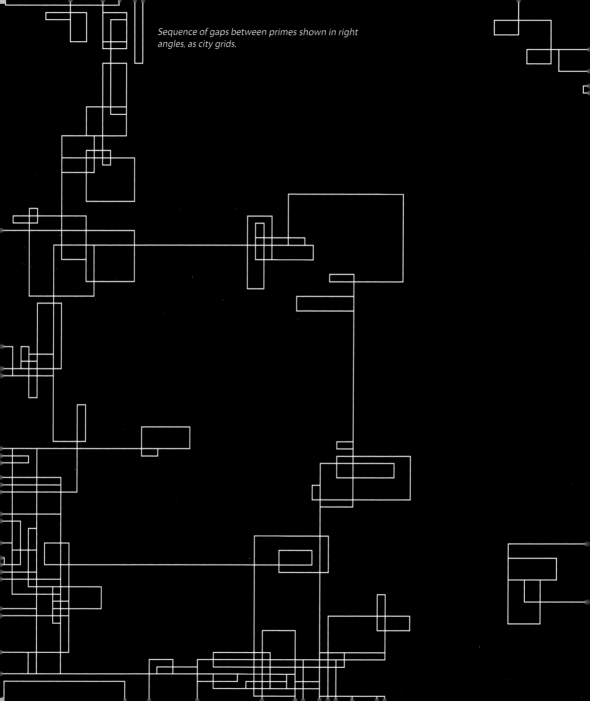

Sequence of gaps between primes shown in right angles, as city grids.

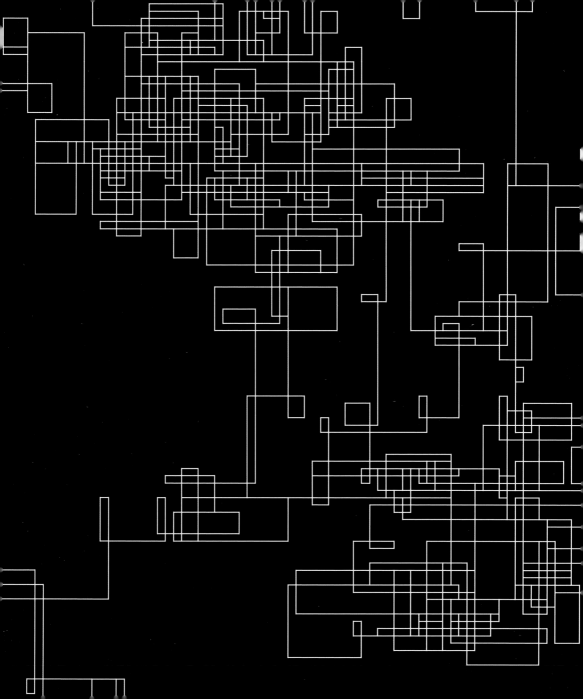

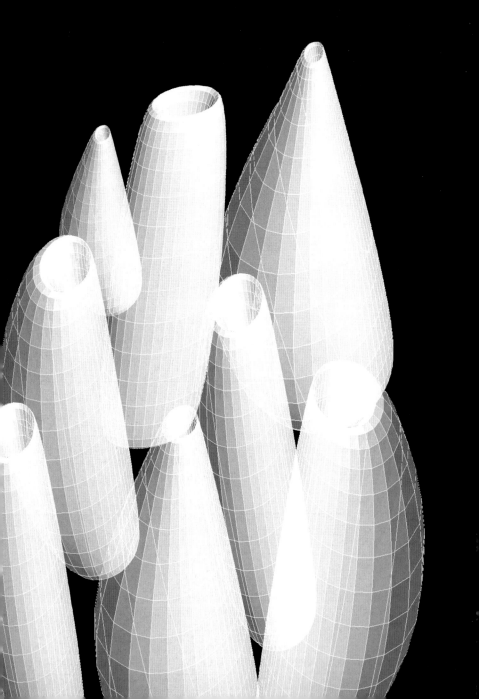

Within the abstract space of numbers the gaps between prime numbers may be seen as a kind of 'tiling', though they open and close at different speeds. Islamic tiling follows more regular rhythms but so wrapped and intricate are the strap-lines of their pattern, that an unending weave seems to take place, moving the eye to travel and not be static. For these artists God is an abstract, not personified, a force in the beauty of rigorous geometry. Patterns within structure the Divine as complex beyond the rules of simple understanding, but underneath is a notion of order and a unifying principle.

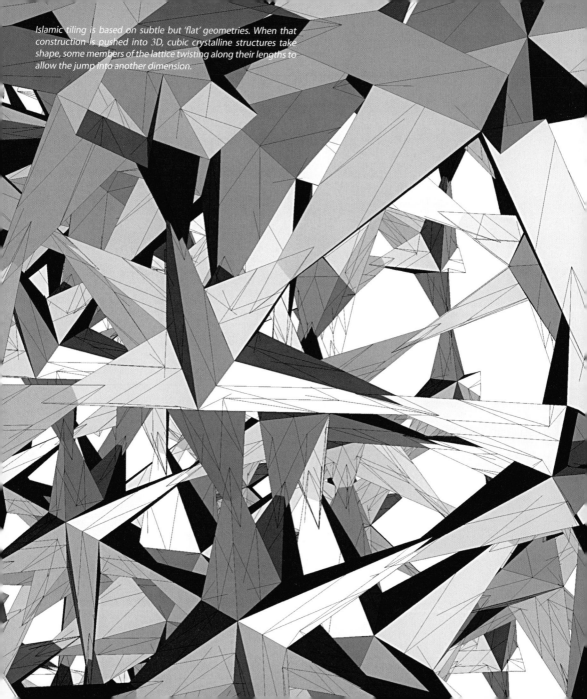

Islamic tiling is based on subtle but 'flat' geometries. When that construction is pushed into 3D, cubic crystalline structures take shape, some members of the lattice twisting along their lengths to allow the jump into another dimension.

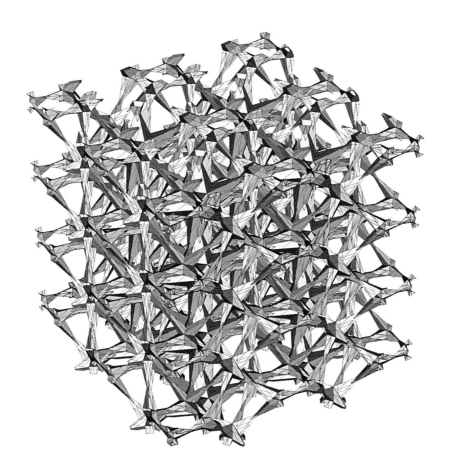

Number is an Element – its value a universal. Beyond emotion and language number is the perfect abstract; it serves as cipher, symbol, and a classification. Ideal for the making of forms, to order and generate sequences that lead to assemblies impossible to think of otherwise, number is a catalyst. With numbers, like the Greeks did once, new architectures may be looked for. They direct magnitude and orientation, take part in proportional constructs and put life into the power of geometry. Numbers give concreteness to a seamless algebra, they also structure the continuum by injecting algorithms with discrete stepping stones.

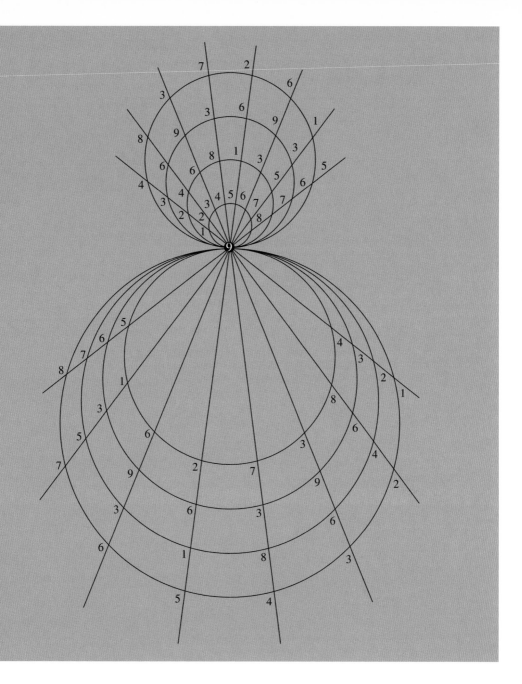

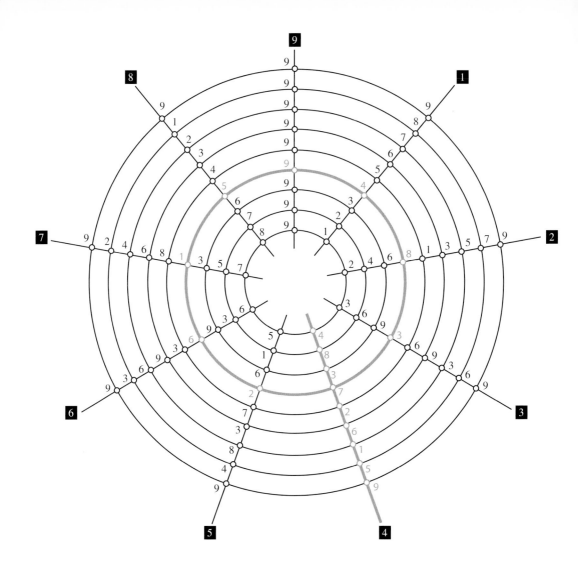

Number nine Mandala – the products of the multiplication tables as single digits arranged in concentric circles, like a Ptolemaic universe.

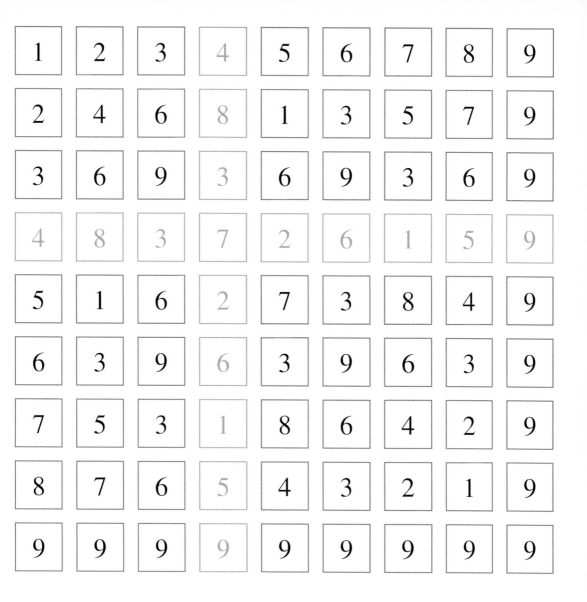

1	2	3	4	5	6	7	8	9
2	4	6	8	1	3	5	7	9
3	6	9	3	6	9	3	6	9
4	8	3	7	2	6	1	5	9
5	1	6	2	7	3	8	4	9
6	3	9	6	3	9	6	3	9
7	5	3	1	8	6	4	2	9
8	7	6	5	4	3	2	1	9
9	9	9	9	9	9	9	9	9

If the products of our multiplication tables are reduced to a single digit (6x6=36 and 3+6 adds up to 9 or 6x8=48 leads to 4+8 adding up to 12, which as 1+2 equals 3) these values may be packed together in a grid, nine by nine, to form a series of interlocked symmetries. There are four reflections within the borders of number 9, the x8 table being the reverse of x1 table, x2 with x7, x3 with x6 and x4 with x5. Like four proteins make up the backbone of the DNA helix our own multiplication tables have a four-stranded power to construct forms. They are like strings of elements, reflective and having reciprocity.

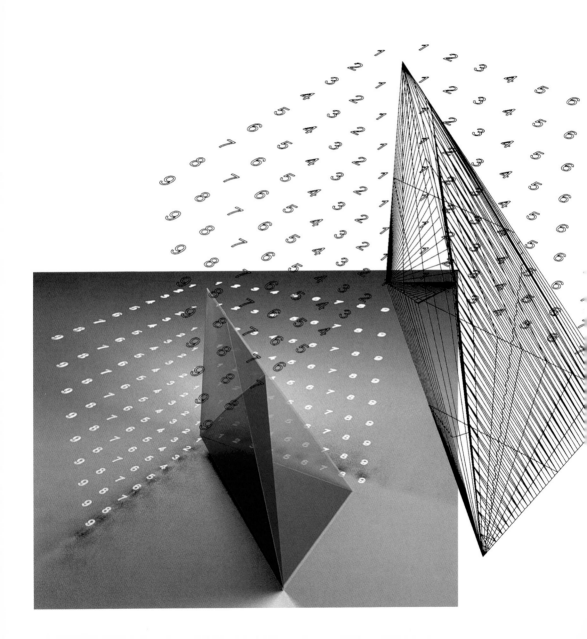

Wire frame and 3D render of 'crystal' made by the array of numbers – from our multiplication tables.

199

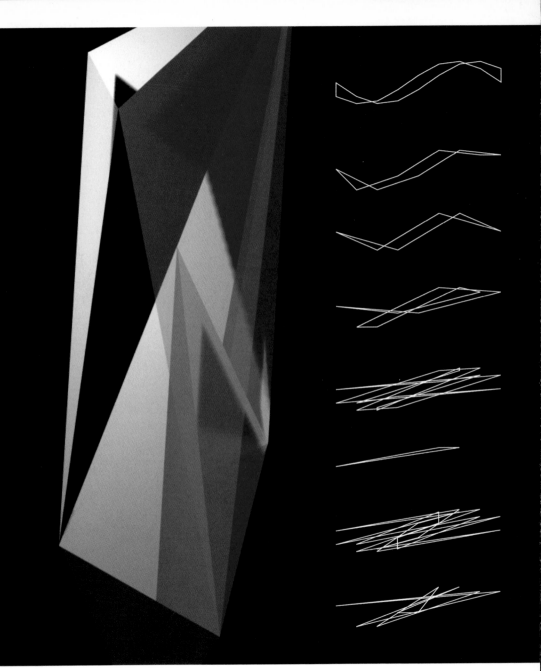

The amorphous runs freely and crystals take the first step towards a definition. When the search lines are straight between potentials then discrete edges mark out the folds, and a crystalline nature.

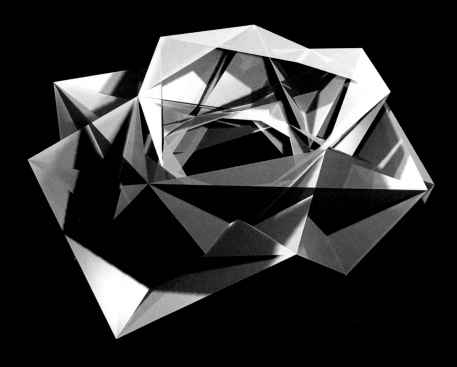

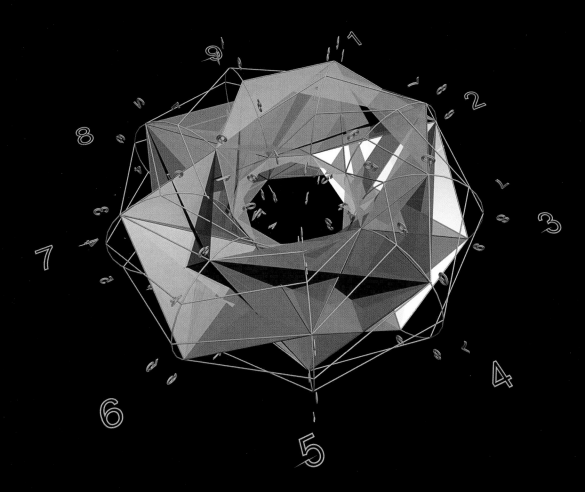

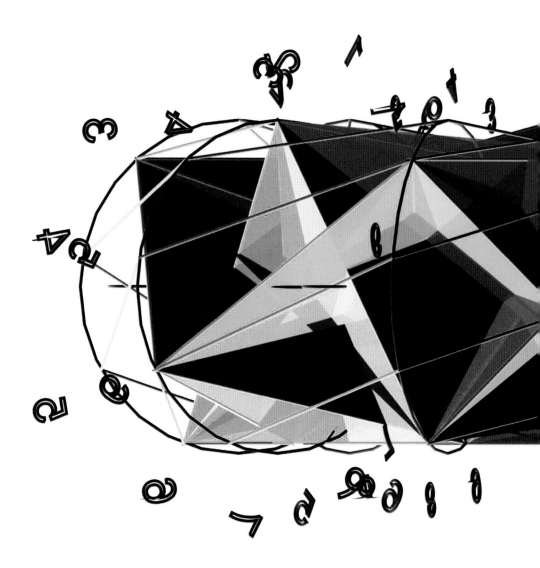

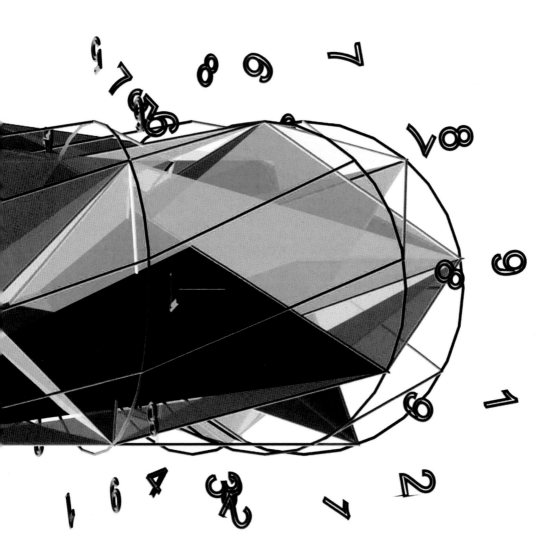

207

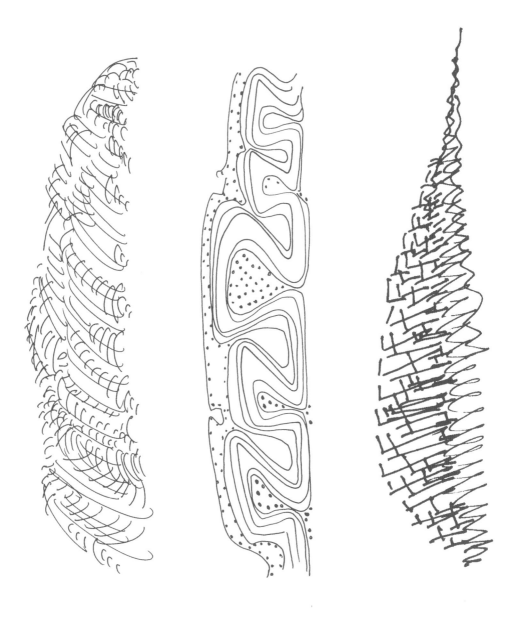

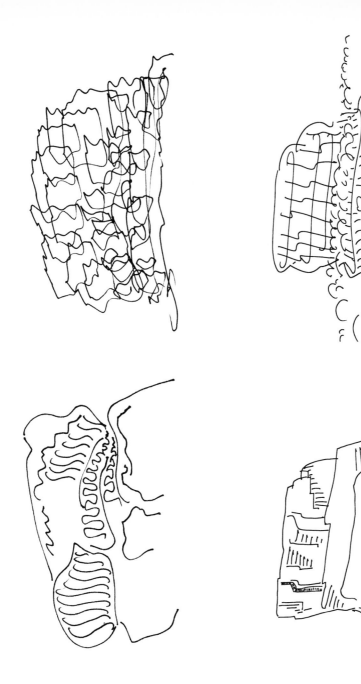

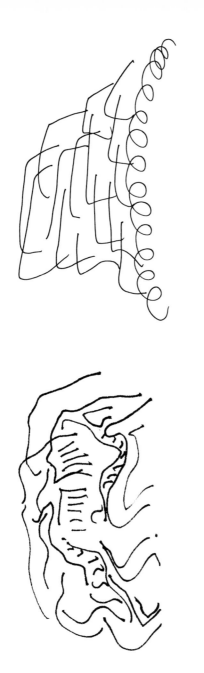

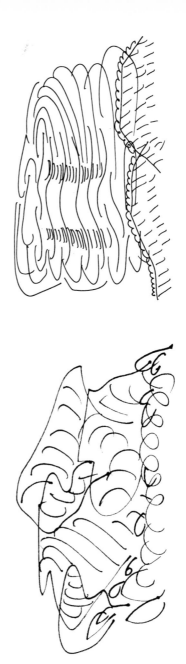

The land was submerged,
covered by a great sea.
Six hundred million years
ago layers of alluvium
flowed into the valley,
part of a vast depression
thousands of square
kilometres in area. Huge
rocks pushed up the planes
and the sea drained away,
alluvium folded, then
crushed and compressed.
Over millions of years
erosions split the layers,
swept them away. What
was left hardened. Flow
marks that once lay
horizontal now inclined to
the vertical, moving down
the sides in slices of smooth
swept waves. What was
buried and yellow in the
quiet underwater is now
exposed, striated, oxidised
red in the baking air.

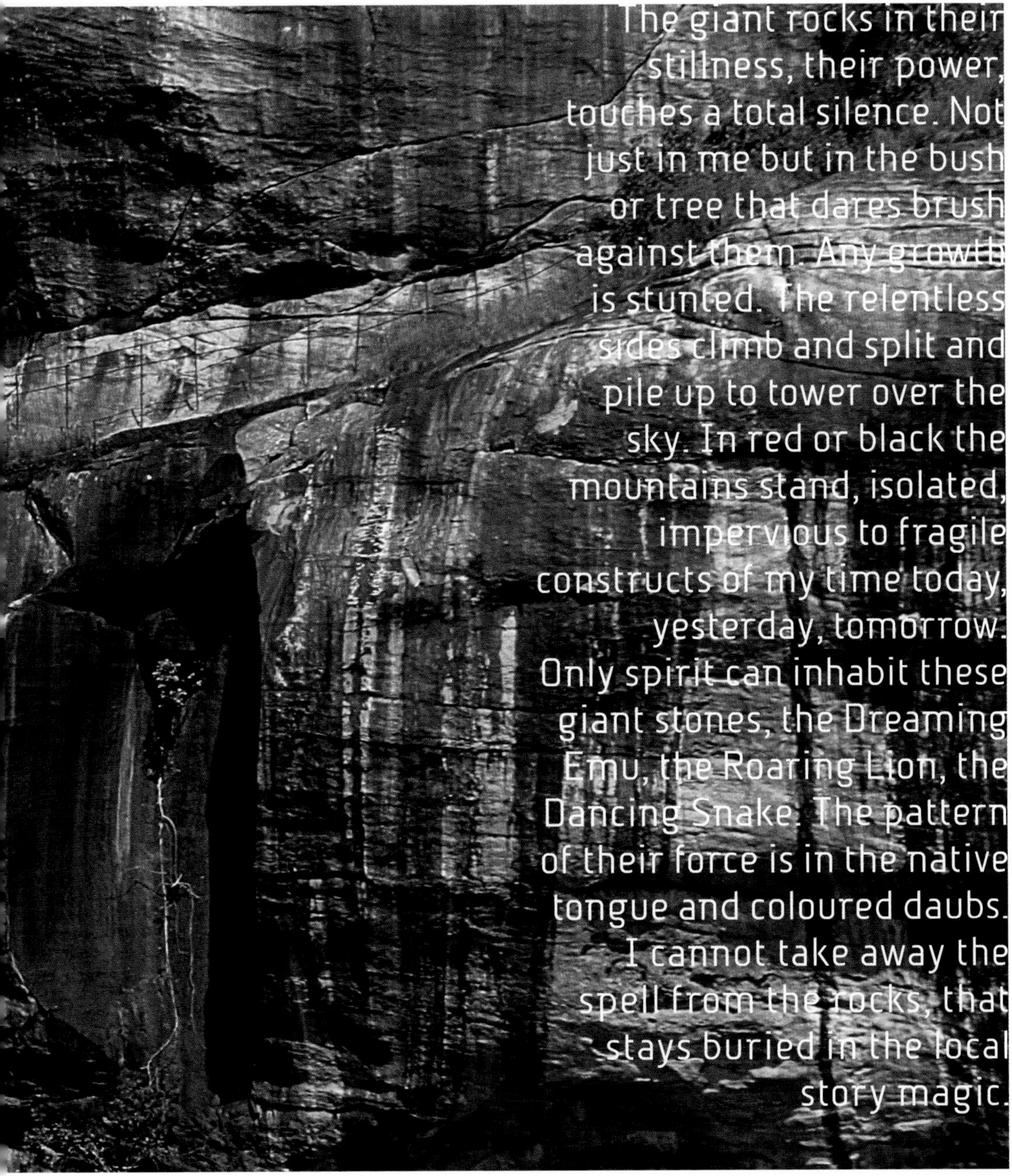

The giant rocks in their
stillness, their power,
touches a total silence. Not
just in me but in the bush
or tree that dares brush
against them. Any growth
is stunted. The relentless
sides climb and split and
pile up to tower over the
sky. In red or black the
mountains stand, isolated,
impervious to fragile
constructs of my time today,
yesterday, tomorrow.
Only spirit can inhabit these
giant stones, the Dreaming
Emu, the Roaring Lion, the
Dancing Snake. The pattern
of their force is in the native
tongue and coloured daubs.
I cannot take away the
spell from the rocks, that
stays buried in the local
story magic.

Wave forms run around the edge of a leaf - within,
the tracery of branch and ever finer branch close up
into cells of nourishment.

Abstract of a leaf – zigzags and dashes,
potentials for the seed of sun,
air, water and earth.

The violent shifts come from the temper of the youngest child on the planet, now seventeen million years old.

Iceland

Mountain streams burst with ice. Water freezes over crevices and on the river bend padded with snow crystals

where the land is pillowed in nightmares. Trapped by the ice, drowned features threaten and stare fixed in the

frozen land. The glacier shifts, slowly. Tons of ice tremble. And fall into the abyss. There it melts in the

depths and fissures, cracks and explodes. The phase shifts – ice to water to steam and back again.

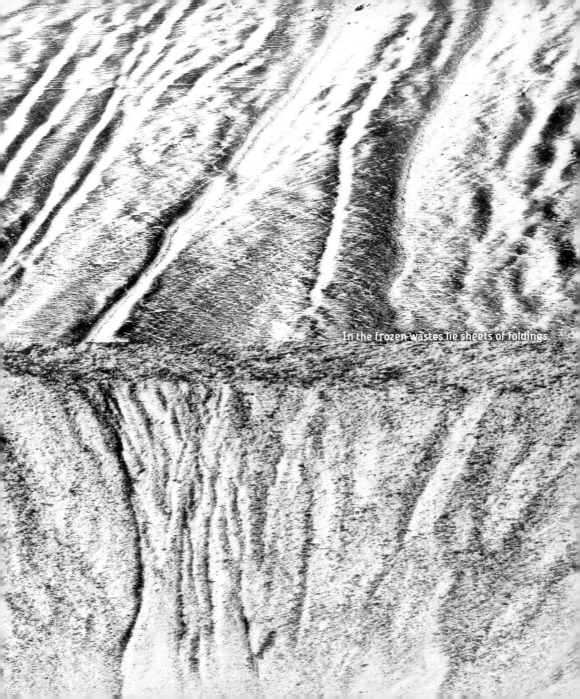

In the frozen wastes lie sheets of foldings

The fall of snow drops settle, consolidate, and become the soft moulds for ice. Under pressure, the loose

packing cannot survive; ice expands, the mould yields, the force buckles the mass. Each fold is a wave with high

branching ridges and troughed valleys. In a land of lava the mountains range black. As the temperature

drops and freezes, snow falls but the rock refuses cover. Against the huge backdrop, dark marks reveal

sketches from a shading pen, as if drawn by giant artists spread around the glacier.

The land that surrounds does
not know us – the dunes,
rocks, vegetation, water and
sun move to a step indifferent
to ours. The cast and mood
of the element is on another
plane. But we cannot stand
apart, we inhabit the domain
and draw from it. The external
invades, intimately. Our mind
seizes the hardness, softness,

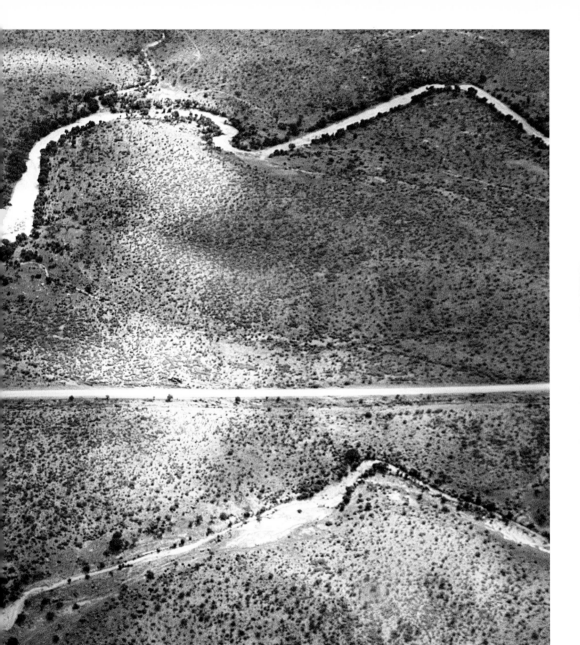

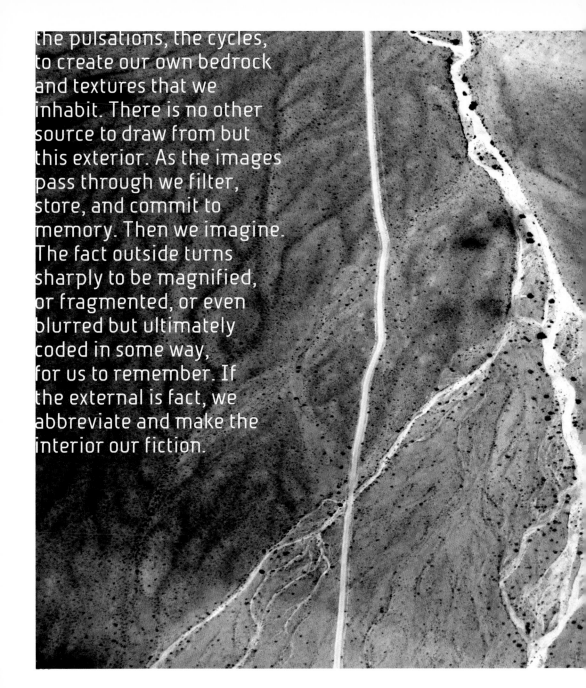

the pulsations, the cycles,
to create our own bedrock
and textures that we
inhabit. There is no other
source to draw from but
this exterior. As the images
pass through we filter,
store, and commit to
memory. Then we imagine.
The fact outside turns
sharply to be magnified,
or fragmented, or even
blurred but ultimately
coded in some way,
for us to remember. If
the external is fact, we
abbreviate and make the
interior our fiction.

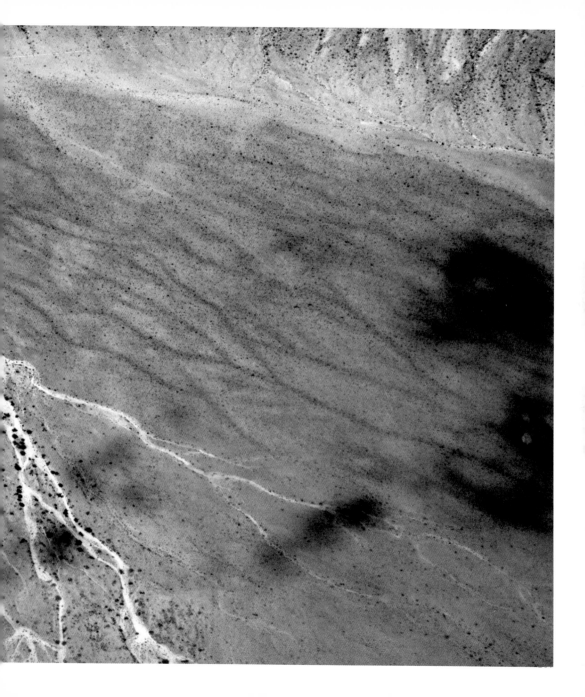

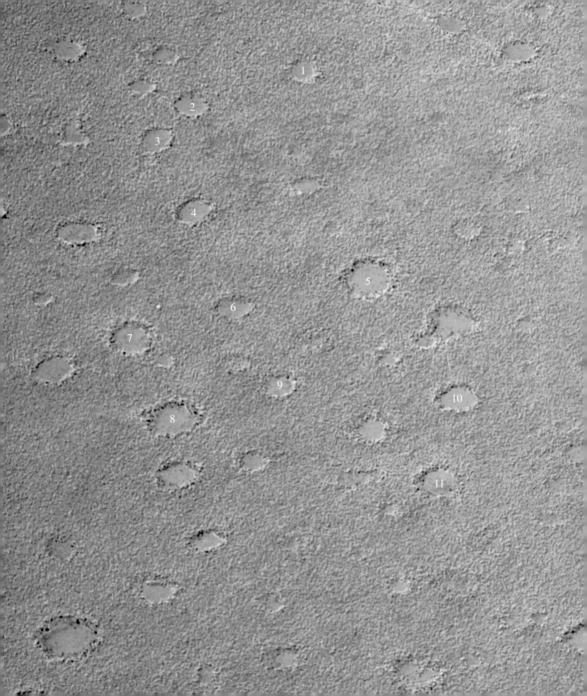

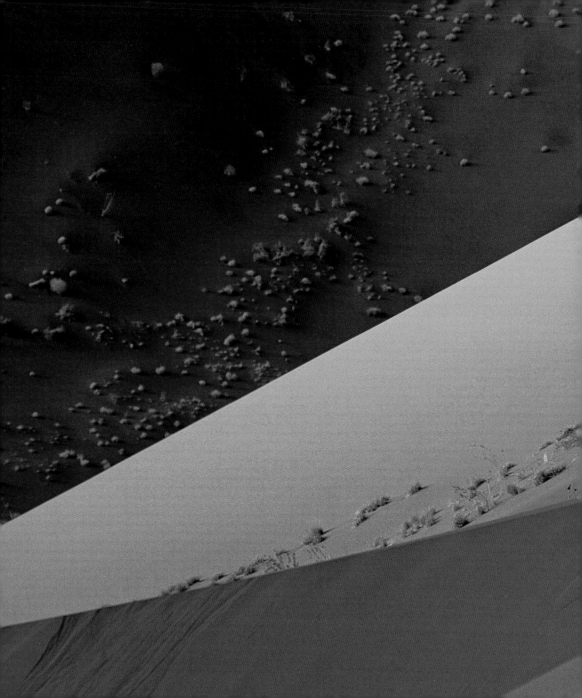

Tell stories to connect with the land. They are more real if the detail is well remembered; not necessarily the exact features but the character of it, the qualities of colour and shadow and location. What makes the telling fresh each time is the bias we put on the observed facts; these facts are wrapped up in patterns – that is why we remember so well and can reinvent the telling. The patterns are codes. We draw and paint them, sing them, write them. The most compressed are the ones we remember for all time, the archetypes, stereotypes, and the mythic structures we create to learn from, and evolve from. To be rich, in the cradle of our imagination, is to be full of stories.

A book grows its own nature; this one began with Kate Mulligan who saw in the material a movement between numbers, nature and architecture. Helping with the design and the graphics, she compiled sections of the book and convinced me to keep going. After she left for other climes Marc Ayala joined me and the design developed, defining more connective tissue – the buildings dropped off, nature and numbers took over. To complete the book I invited Fruitmachine to advise on structure plus inject a smart typography. They saw a cycle in the material and proposed a split cover and, uniquely, a rotating book. This did not quite happen the way we anticipated but the insight helped the overall layout. I owe huge thanks to William Coggan who stayed with many edits and kept faith in the texts as they slowly took shape. I am grateful for the steady support of the Prestel team of Jürgen Krieger, Katharina Haderer and to Curt Holtz for the close collaboration on editorial matters. Sarah, my daughter, advised on the essay and special thanks to my son John for the wonderful photographs of the Namibian desert, which are a highlight of the book. As always, I have an inspired team to work with in the Arup AGU and must mention Daniel Bosia/Francis Archer for their work on aperiodic tiling. Thanks to my family, who again allowed the imposition of a book to intrude into our household and who supported me throughout.

This book is dedicated to Shirley, John, Sarah, James.

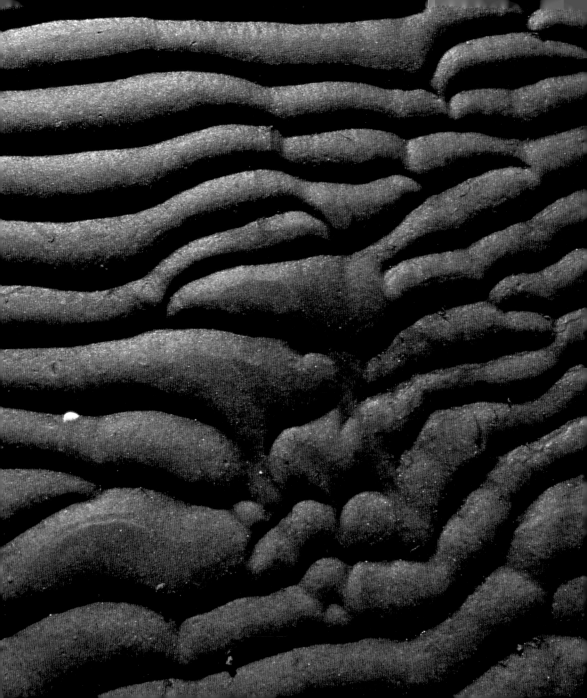

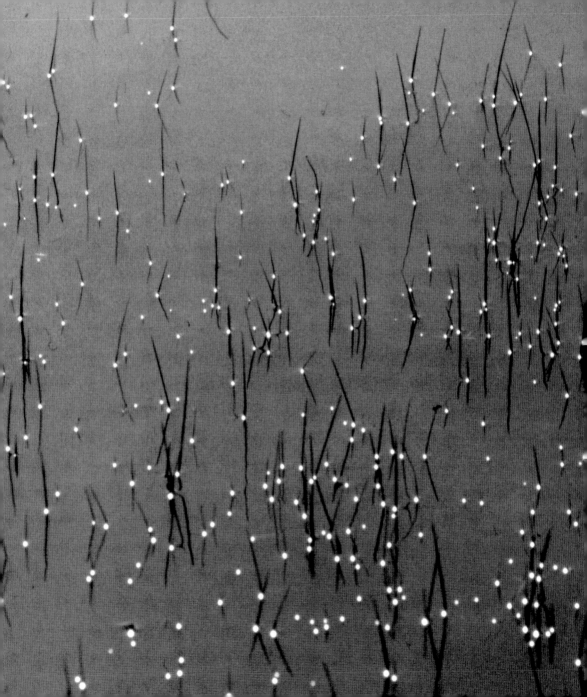

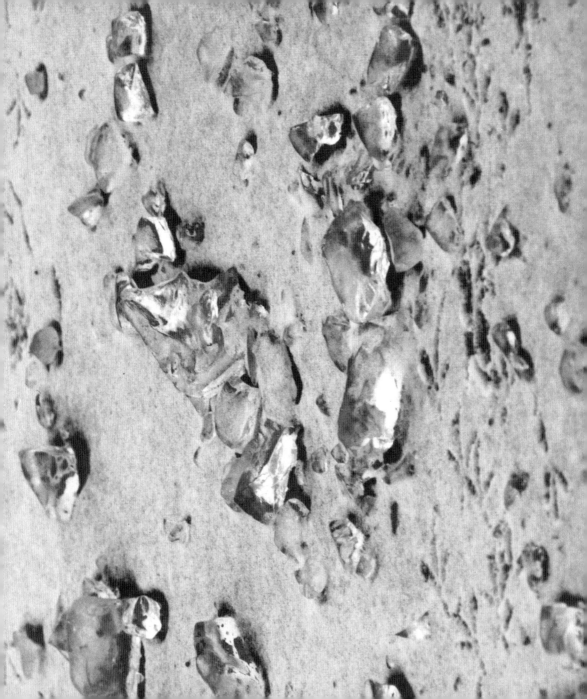

Template:

A template serves as a model, it is used as a pattern for cutting, shaping or drilling: in biochemistry – a nucleic acid molecule that acts as a pattern for the sequence of assembly of a protein or other large molecule. A template hides tempo, the pace at which an activity or process takes place, dependent on the density of material. A template is a catalyst for action.

From the largest to the smallest scale the void is filled with powerful forces, attractors and repulsors. In the uncertainty are delicate structures of chance – of what might be. A sudden concentration, and a potential turns to fact. Something begins to happen. The bias sets a trend. If this is birth in the physical, the world of our nature has even more starts, in the virtual. Our imaginings of what might be are pure sorcery. We may look at a plant and reduce its material to a few marks, and gazing upon those abstract values we may see other patterns; away from the leaf we chase a wider network. If we extract the patterns we may code them and use mathematics. And then we could travel to the most hallucinatory of dimensions, all it takes is algebra and geometry. Put an x or y into the equation based on a diagram, where the variable has infinite range, and every outcome is possible.

The chemistry of the sign takes us into the meta-physics of a non-real world but all the more real because there's more to it than the 3D-eye can possibly see.

Because we see how things are it does not mean that we know what anything is. Each of us can speculate but we must rely on insight; a poem has something to do with it. Poetry has inner rhythms, conflicts and dissonances. Its deep structure is non-linear, full of juxtaposition and clashes. Layering leads to ambiguity; interpretation is the only key to the original imagination. Is not this like nature?

If we dig deeper and search for connections relationships are found. What is below and abstracted seems to be more fundamental. Much is gained by working from in to out.

We speculate, we make. And when we make, we run far to speculate as to what is the object just made? Between the exterior fact and an interior ghost, a subversive loop – feedback – primes and structures a surrendering imagination. The 'Real' has no compartmentation but is a matrix of a few facts embedded in a much larger virtual; it is full of holes.

Pattern is catalyst, a template for action between an idea and its event and, in reverse, between the reality and the metaphor that arises out of such concreteness.

Pattern is multi-layered. (Like a person has a basic body signature; then limbs and fingers in successive proportional growths, with small features like nails and eyelashes for further detail.)

But the belief in streamlining has brought about a stripped-down reality. Ornamentation and embellishment has been forgotten. In an idea like branching, taken to several scales tufted with buds and leaves, the leaves in turn showing bifurcations great and small, the form is more a network than a fixed entity – it keeps growing, or dies. The seed algorithm promotes the basic idea, of branching, at several scales, and the environment feeds the chance for variation, stunted, normal, or exaggerated.

We are compelled to create, as part of a natural condition. Being immersed in patterns we navigate between surface layers and the codes hidden behind them. Imagining complex features we draw the simple diagram, relying on the power of pattern or maths, to code and interpret. The mind does not 'know' but instinctively searches, to extend its own forms. To create a new fact is more like a prophecy about our mind than revelation.

What appears confused in a jumble suddenly changes into relevance when the pieces fit together. Order is found where there was none before. Puzzling out a solution – we seem to like doing that – and if it's just for its own sake the study seems to be even more rewarding. How does uselessness give pleasure so easily? Maybe because beauty lurks in the 'purity' of something; the less attached and meaningful the more beautiful? So we chase theory for its own sake.

Geometry advances when it is a movement for change, making a network rather than a static map. In a network the choice is being made on the basis of which way to read the message or data? (Structure lies in the answer – there are many structures.) And geometry advances when its connections and network are part of an evolving pattern, when it ceases to be static.

pattern, styles and fashions
geometry, regulates and forms
structure, proportions and constructs

Volume is a dimension harder won than surface, the cube takes more effort than the square. Surface wants to extend and spread but volume pulls back to confine. When surface spreads pattern tends to dominate; but with volume, materiality and substance is defined. The balance between surface and volume is critical for survival.

Shape is STATIC.   Form is DYNAMIC.

There is always tension between Form and Shape and between Volume and Surface. Balancing pattern with substance is the pivot of a new aesthetic. Too much pattern and the artefact or event remains decorative. Too much substance, so that the pattern is lost, leads to deformation and loss of inspiration. The just-right balance is for pattern and substance to not sacrifice each other. Nature does this well, in a fit-for-purpose battle. The idea, the code or instruction, keeps being read as the flesh of it gets eaten up but not to excess, one way or the other – when that happens grotesques occur, they die. A design learns from this process. When we get it right we find the work beautiful. However mixed up to the eye at first glance and complex, a rigour behind the surface will make connections, point to deeper symmetry. The rate of progress of one trend balances against the other – push and pull. The intrigue lies in the check of openness against the pull of control. In perfect symmetry, everything reflects the other, no direction is found. As a figure or object centres upon itself, then, the contemplation is static – but deep symmetry is full of symmetry breaking.

Imagine the galaxy and its spiral arms and the scatter of stardust – there is large variance, but about an axis through the Universe the angular momentum is constant. The product of mass times angular velocity for the cosmos about a line does not vary from time to time; that is why equilibrium and balance happen, and things don't fly apart. Everything is changing as galaxies spread and new ones are born but the calculation of masses involved with rotation somehow manages to stay constant. In the Law of Angular Momentum conservation is at work – a rule that repeats. There need be no superficial symmetry – but a changing mix that hides a shifting rule of order.

Materiality is information. Data!

Gathered in sequence or connected up through networks, data nodes out structures of communication. Geometry is implied in this model.

Data has value but to keep one value distinct from another means a strategy for differentiation. In physical objects this is the generation of space geometry – material can only be spaced apart by geometry. The algebra of the continuous is bridged to the arithmetic of the discrete by the geometries of pattern.

material arises out of energy (e=mc²)
connectivity out of materiality
geometry out of connectivity
structure out of geometry
form out of structure
the void out of form

The universe succeeds because its structures accumulate through repetition, and they can be compressed into code; mathematics best describes the patterns. The graph of a circle is produced by the equation $x^2+y^2=r^2$ (r is the radius and x and y are values along axes at right angles to each other). Millions of circles are possible by adjusting r from value 1 to infinity. The pattern $x^2+y^2=r^2$ is a concentric template of all possible circles. What we see on the surface are the many but underneath is one model.

Below the integer counting of protons and neutrons there are fractions to the energy, which are the substances of the quarks and mesons, sub-atomic particles. Below these units, more like mathematical entities at this level of paring, matter is viewed as superstrings or quantum loops. Is material ultimately a mathematical sense of information?

The possible is made by chance, locally. There is no certainty of outcome, only a hope of prediction. The more likely an outcome the higher the confidence limit, but nothing is certain. The diagram of such chance is tree-like, a diagram of branching contingencies; if this happens, then that happens; we go from one split to another, taking a chance. The actual structure of what happens is a series of forked paths through an intangible forest. What is surprising is that a start with the roll of dice, by feedback and repeat throws, emerges towards a structure that does take form.

'Order' is really latent chaos – the 'fact' that may be pulled apart by the next chance, but not yet tripped up by the path taken so far.

Space has random starts. As the geometry or algebra repeats, by aggregation a form grows. Complexity arises. Any 'answer' picked out is a frozen instant. The pictures are scaleless. Resulting maps could be labelled universe, landscape, villa, piece of furniture. A form is emergent but the connectivity, at a particular scale, limits the material choice.

In a primordial ocean of all possibilities a current of the random strikes – chance! Concrete fact materialises. More strikes and a stability arises. In the solid fact is the seed of the improbability that began it all, so nothing may last. For at the origin, nothing was certain. That is why we look out for pattern, it outlasts the construct.

Index

Index

Cecil Balmond was born in Sri Lanka in 1943 and is a designer and structural engineer of world renown. He is Deputy Chairman of Ove Arup and Partners Ltd. and leads a unit of scientists, architects and engineers to pursue his interest in the genesis of form using numbers, music and mathematics as vital sources.

He has collaborated with the world's leading architects and artists including Rem Koolhaas, Toyo Ito, Daniel Libeskind and Anish Kapoor. His critically acclaimed footbridge in Coimbra, Portugal, was completed in 2006.

Balmond is the author of *Number 9 – The Search for the Sigma Code* (1998) and *informal* (2002), both published by Prestel. He has received many awards for his work including the Gengo Matsui Prize and the RIBA Charles Jencks Award for Theory in Practice. He has taught at Harvard GSD and at the Yale School of Architecture and he now holds the Crét Chair at PennDesign as Professor of Architecture.

Prestel Verlag
Königinstrasse 9
80539 Munich
Tel. +49 (89) 24 29 08-0
Fax +49 (89) 24 29 08-335

Prestel Publishing Ltd.
4 Bloomsbury Place
London WC1A 2QA
Tel. +44 (0) 20 7323-5004
Fax +44 (0) 20 7636-8004

Prestel Publishing
900 Broadway, Suite 603
New York, N.Y. 10003
Tel. +1 (212) 995-2720
Fax +1 (212) 995-2733

www.prestel.com

Prestel books are available worldwide. Please contact your
nearest bookseller or one of the above addresses for information
concerning your local distributor.

Library of Congress Control Number: 2006939120

British Library Cataloguing-in-Publication Data: a catalogue
record for this book is available from the British Library.
The Deutsche Bibliothek holds a record of this publication in the
Deutsche Nationalbibliografie; detailed bibliographical data can
be found under: http://dnb.ddb.de

Editorial direction by Curt Holtz
Design and layout by Marc Ayala; Fruitmachine, London
Origination by Reproline Mediateam, Munich
Printed and bound by Druckerei Uhl, Radolfzell

Printed in Germany on acid-free paper

ISBN 978-3-7913-3778-4